CRIMINAL SENTENCES

CRIMINAL SENTENCES

DANIEL KELLY
LL.B.(Hons.)(Edin.), Cert. de H. Et. Eur. (Bruges)
Advocate

T&T CLARK
EDINBURGH

T&T CLARK LTD
59 GEORGE STREET
EDINBURGH EH2 2LQ
SCOTLAND

ISBN 0 567 29240 1

First published 1993

British Library Cataloguing-in-Publication Data
A catalogue record for this book is available
from the British Library

Typeset by Buccleuch Printers Ltd, Hawick
Printed and bound in Great Britain by Redwood Books, Wiltshire

INTRODUCTION

The oft-mooted assertion that there is no sentencing policy in Scotland presents a challenge to ascertain the extent to which a coherent sentencing system may be discerned. An examination of the decisions of the High Court of Justiciary over the past decade or so reveals that although there may not be any *guidelines* on sentencing, there is a considerable amount of *guidance* available on sentencing. It is almost axiomatic to say that each case depends upon its own facts and circumstances and that no pre-established sentence can be applied in respect of a particular offence. Were that not the case, there would be no need for sentencers. Yet, no sentence is pronounced in a vacuum and it is essential for sentencers as well as for others involved, particularly those acting on behalf of an offender, to be aware of what has been said in similar cases.

In those countries with more rigid sentencing policies attempts have been made to analyse current sentencing practice. In a similar way, an attempt may be made, through an examination of the workings of the Court of Criminal Appeal in sentencing cases, to draw together the court's decisions and to present an overview of current sentencing practice in Scotland.

Incorporated in Part One are those general observations on sentencing which can be taken from the decisions of the Court of Criminal Appeal. Also included are references to the relevant statutory provisions on sentencing. Part Two contains notes on specific offences, generally where the Court of Criminal Appeal has been asked to consider whether a sentence was excessive. While these cases are not to be taken as tariffs for the particular offences, the sentence for a specific offence being left to the discretion of the sentencer, an indication may be gleaned from them of the levels of sentence which have or have not in the past been deemed to be excessive. Moreover, in certain instances in the course o individual cases the appeal court has made observations which have a general application to sentencing practice in similar cases. Such general observations on aspects of sentencing and in relation to specific offences when brought together and added to the appropriate statutory provisions do in effect make up a significant sentencing framework in Scotland.

Although the book is intended primarily for lawyers it may also be of interest to those in other professions such as social workers.

I would like to express my thanks to my wife, Christine, for her assistance and to Robert Shiels for reading and commenting on a draft of the text.

Advocates Library
Edinburgh
January 1993

CONTENTS

PART TWO

TABLE OF CASES

TABLE OF STATUTES

PART ONE

CHAPTER 1

SENTENCING PRINCIPLES

1.1 Introduction

Although there may not be any overall framework of sentencing principles in Scotland, there are several provisions, rulings and practices which do have a general application to the sentence which may be imposed in any individual case. Certain general rules regarding sentencing are to be found in legislative provisions. To these may be added those observations of general import which have been made in the course of decisions of the Court of Criminal Appeal. The Court of Criminal Appeal, which is the High Court of Justiciary in its appellate capacity, sits in Edinburgh and consists of three or more High Commissioners of Justiciary, frequently presided over by the Lord Justice-General or the Lord Justice-Clerk. It has to deal with an increasing number of appeals against sentence and many of the more significant cases have been reported. A number of these general sentencing provisions, rulings and practices are drawn together in this chapter.

1.2 Responsibility of the judge

It is a fundamental principle that the trial judge must decide upon the appropriate sentence in each case. The responsibility for what the sentence should be is his and his alone. This has been said to be a rule which should not be impaired in any way whatsoever.[1]

1.3 First offender

The fact that a person has not previously offended is a very important factor in determining sentence.[2] Special considerations apply before a first custodial sentence may be imposed.[3] This may be seen more as a rule of general practice than as any sentencing principle.

It is only in an exceptional case that the maximum penalty could properly be imposed upon a first offender. Thus, where a sheriff imposed the maximum fines on a first offender after a trial in his absence on the ground that there were no mitigating factors placed before the court, the fines were quashed and more moderate fines were imposed.[4] In imposing a fine the court should not have regard to its power to remit a fine in whole or in part and impose a high fine on the basis that the offender can subsequently seek to have it remitted.

Regardless of whether a person has appeared before a children's panel, when he appears before a court for the first time he is a first offender and entitled to be treated as such. This would also be the case if a person appeared for the first time on a complaint or indictment containing numerous charges.[5] However, although earlier bad behaviour as a child does not affect a person's status as a first offender, it may be relevant in selecting an appropriate sentence.[6]

1.4   Comparative justice principle

1.4.1 General. In imposing sentence on more than one offender, the court should strive to achieve comparative justice between them. For example, where two persons convicted of theft of over £4,000 were each sentenced to four years' imprisonment, one having been previously fined small sums on two charges of theft, two of breach of the peace and two of assault, the other having eight previous convictions on which he had received terms of imprisonment of up to seven years, in the interests of comparative justice, having regard to the differences in their histories, the former's sentence was reduced to one of three years' imprisonment.[7]

The court is prepared to apply the comparative justice principle to cases where accused persons are convicted of different offences, provided they are closely related. Where two persons appeared on the same complaint concerning offences committed during a trade war between factions of ice-cream traders, the principle was applied. The sheriff had fined one offender for reckless driving while imprisoning a second for damaging a window of a mobile shop. As no apparent reason was given for the different ways of sentencing the two, the prison sentence was quashed and a fine substituted.[8]

The principle was similarly applied where one of three co-accused pled guilty and gave evidence against the other two. After they had been convicted, all three were remitted to the High Court of Justiciary for sentence. Of the other co-accused, one with a bad record was sentenced to five years' imprisonment and the other who had very little record to four years' imprisonment. Also having very little record, the original one was sentenced to three years' detention and had to be placed in protective custody because he had been threatened. On appeal, the court considered that insufficient account had been taken of the distinction between him and his co-accused, of his co-operation with the Crown and of his sentence being more onerous because he was in protective custody and his sentence was reduced to two years' detention.[9]

Insufficient attention was paid to the comparative justice principle where two people were convicted of reset, one also being convicted of a breach of bail. The one convicted of reset only, a first offender with a very small income, was fined £200. The other was fined £300 in cumulo. He had "a record almost as long as your arm involving criminality of all kinds, including many offences of dishonesty and, in recent years, even a conviction for fraud". In addition, he was on bail. By comparison, the fine of £200 imposed on the first offender was excessive. It was therefore quashed and a fine of £100 was imposed.[10]

The comparative justice principle had not been properly applied in an assault case where two co-accused with bad records for assault were sentenced to six months' imprisonment and the third offender, who had previously been imprisoned for road traffic offences but had no previous convictions for assault, was sentenced to three months' imprisonment. As the sheriff had not attached sufficient weight to the fact that the third's record was not nearly as bad as that of his co-accused, his sentence was quashed and fines amounting to £250 imposed.[11]

Consideration must also be given to the effect of backdating a sentence and to any period already spent in prison on remand. Where the more serious of two offenders was sentenced to nine months' detention, backdated, and the other offender was sentenced to six months' detention from the date when sentence was imposed, even although he had spent three months in custody on remand before being granted bail, the effect was that the more serious offender received a less severe sentence. In order to restore the balance, a sentence of three months' detention was substituted for the less serious offender.[12]

Although the courts would still be expected to achieve comparative justice as between offenders, a failure to do so will not necessarily result in a successful appeal against sentence. The fact that too low a sentence is imposed upon one co-accused is not in itself considered by the Court of Criminal Appeal to be a ground for interfering with the sentence imposed on another co-accused. The question to be posed is whether the sentence imposed upon the offender was an appropriate one in the circumstances. If it was, the fact that too low a sentence was imposed on one co-accused would not be regarded as a reason for altering the correct sentence imposed on another co-accused.[13] Thus, if the sentence could not in itself be regarded as excessive, even although another judge might have differentiated between the co-acccused, the Court of Criminal Appeal will not interfere with the sentence.[14]

1.4.2 Different judges. Where sentences are imposed by different judges and one is uncertain of all the detail which had been put before the other judge, it is not possible to draw any reliable comparison between the sentences imposed. Moreover, if one judge concludes that the sentence imposed by another judge upon a co-accused is a light sentence, the sentencing judge is not obliged to impose upon the accused appearing before him a sentence which he believes is inadequate. The judge has to determine what would be the appropriate sentence to impose in respect of that offence.[15]

1.5 Exemplary sentence

There are occasions when a court may wish to impose an exemplary sentence. By implication, all indictments conclude with the words that the accused "ought to be punished with the pains of law to deter others from committing the like crimes in all time coming".[16] The appeal court has on occasion congratulated a sheriff for his selection of penalties, as when one imposed an exemplary penalty for a thoroughly bad case of reckless driving where there was an increasing frequency of analogous offences within the sheriffdom.[17]

A sheriff was held to be entitled to disqualify a first offender who failed to stop after an accident when that offence had become prevalent in the area and the public's attention had frequently been drawn to the fact that it may well result in a disqualification.[18] An exemplary sentence was approved on someone who committed two unprovoked assaults while he was drunk following a football match. Although he was a first offender and the victims had no real injuries, he had been fined £100 on each charge. The appeal court commented: "People who commit offences of this kind are public pests and the sheriff was absolutely right to do what he did."[19] A sentence of six months' imprisonment for the first charge of possessing cocaine in the jurisdiction, which was imposed in the hope of deterring others, has also been upheld.[20]

In other cases exemplary sentences have been deemed to be inappropriate. In one instance a sheriff fined a hospital nurse £500 for assaulting a mental patient by standing on his arms and legs.[21] The fine contained an element of exemplary sentence since the offender was the senior person in the ward, with considerable experience, and what he did had shocked less experienced nurses and had disgusted one. The appeal court took a different view. As no injury was caused, the conviction would have had consequences for the offender's career and there were no previous convictions, it considered that there was no room for the imposition of an exemplary sentence. The fine was quashed and one of £50 substituted.

Although it may be appropriate to impose an exemplary sentence for a serious offence, the court should also have regard to the appropriateness of imposing it on the particular offender before it. A judge selected the wrong person on whom to impose an exemplary sentence when the individual was someone who had not significantly offended before.[22]

1.6 Cumulo sentence

A court has power where several charges at common law or under any statute or order are embraced in one indictment or complaint to impose a cumulo fine in respect of all or any of the charges of which the accused is convicted.[23] Although the statutory provision deals with fines, cumulo sentences of imprisonment have also been imposed in practice. While that might be justified in some cases, on occasion it could lead to problems. Courts should therefore consider very carefully whether it is appropriate in any particular case to impose a cumulo sentence.

In cases where more than one statutory offence is libelled it has been said to be desirable that on conviction the court should impose a sentence on each of the charges.[24] Unless that is done, difficulties may arise in a subsequent appeal in the event of the conviction on some of the charges being quashed. Whether the charges are statutory or at common law, courts should be careful not to impose a cumulo sentence if there is any risk of problems occurring in a subsequent appeal. Where sentence is to be imposed on a number of charges, unless it is clear that in the event of an appeal all of the charges will stand or fall together, separate sentences should be imposed in respect of each charge.[25]

A cumulo sentence of imprisonment could not be imposed if imprisonment was not competent for one of the offences charged in the first instance.[26] A cumulo sentence of imprisonment for several breaches of a statutory provision which exceeded the limit of imprisonment provided by the statute would be incompetent.[27] However, a judge is entitled to impose a cumulo fine in respect of a number of offences which exceeds the maximum provided by the statutes for a single offence.[28]

1.7   Double sentencing

In arriving at an appropriate sentence, it would be contrary to principle for a judge to take into account other charges in respect of which separate sentences had been imposed. For example, when considering the recklessness or degree of danger of a person's driving, it would punish the person twice to take into account aspects of his driving for which he had already been sentenced, such as where he had also been convicted of driving at the same time with an excess of alcohol.[29]

1.8   Plea of guilty

It is generally irrelevant for sentencing purposes whether an accused pleads guilty or not guilty. A discount should not be given from what would otherwise be the appropriate sentence for an early plea of guilty. This would involve a form of plea-bargaining. It follows from the presumption of innocence that an accused person is entitled to go to trial and leave the Crown to establish his guilt if it can do so. An accused person should not be put in the position of realising that if he pleads guilty early enough he will receive a lower sentence than he would otherwise receive. Moreover, to operate a discount policy would disable the judge from exercising his discretion fully and freely in a particular case.[30]

Sparing children the further pain of having to give evidence may be a factor in restricting the sentence imposed.[31]

1.9 Views of the victim

It may be legitimate to enquire into certain objective matters of fact which might indicate the attitude of the victim subsequent to the offence. For example, there might previously have been a close relationship between the offender and the victim, such as in the case of a husband and wife, and it might be relevant that they had reconciled. However, it is entirely wrong that the victim should be asked for his or her views on the basis that what he or she may say might affect the ultimate disposal of the case. The victim would not know of the possible disposals or the appropriate sentencing principles. Any comments would have no relevance to the decision which the court and the court alone must take.[32]

1.10 Role of the Crown

The Crown has no role or interest in the actual sentencing process itself. Nothing should be done to weaken this principle by requiring the Crown to participate in the process.[33] However, were a judge to exceed his powers or to impose an incompetent sentence, if aware of it the prosecutor would be expected to bring this to the attention of the court.

1.11 Art and part involvement

A person may be convicted of and punished for a contravention of any enactment notwithstanding that he was guilty of such contravention as art and part only. Any person who aids, abets, counsels, procures or incites any other person to commit an offence against the provisions of any enactment is guilty of an offence and is liable on conviction, unless the enactment otherwise requires, to the same punishment as might be imposed on conviction of the offence.[34]

The particular role played in a conspiracy by one of a team of offenders is not necessarily relevant when it comes to sentencing that individual. When a team enterprise takes place, the courts recognise that roles are allotted to the various participants and it does not matter whether an individual's role is a leading, supporting or character role. The essential point is that the event took place as a team enterprise and the sentence should be appropriate to that enterprise.[35]

1.12 Bail

For sentencing purposes, it is irrelevant that a person in breach of bail is ultimately acquitted of the charges for which he has been on bail.[36]

To impose the maximum sentence for the first time that an accused person contravenes s. 3 of the Bail etc. (Scotland) Act 1980 is, save in the most exceptional circumstances, to impose an excessive sentence.[37] However, the maximum sentence of three months' imprisonment for someone with no previous convictions for breach of bail was upheld where the offender had committed three serious drugs offences while on bail.[38]

Sentences imposed for contravention of the Bail Act should normally be made consecutive to any sentences imposed in respect of other charges on the same complaint or indictment. It is competent for a judge to order the sentences in respect of contraventions of several bail orders to run consecutively.[39]

1.13 Children

1.13.1 General. It is presumed in Scotland that children below the age of eight cannot be guilty of an offence.[40] However, the appeal court has had to decide whether children as young as eight should be the subject of a custodial disposal.[41]

A child may be ordered to be detained and while so detained is deemed to be in legal custody.[42] In considering a disposal the court will have to weigh the advantages and disadvantages of custodial as opposed to domiciliary supervision and also have regard to the public interest.[43] In the period to 1991 about thirty children had been sentenced to periods of detention in solemn cases under the current legislation.[44]

The words "conviction" and "sentence" should not be used in relation to children dealt with summarily. A finding of guilt is made in respect of a child rather than a conviction being recorded and an order is made upon that finding rather than a sentence being imposed.[45]

1.13.2 Parent. For the sole reason of the effect which a prison sentence would have on a mother's young children, in particular on a baby of 10 months, the appeal court has reduced a period of imprisonment imposed on the mother from four to three years.[46]

1.14 Delay between offence and sentence
A change of circumstances between the date when a person should have appeared in court and when he actually did appear should not be considered in determining sentence. Where there was a delay of 15 months in the execution of a warrant due to the accused person absconding, it was decided that the court should look at the accused person's position when he should have appeared, the delay having been entirely due to his own conduct.[47]

1.15 Extraneous matters
Clearly, extraneous matters should not be taken into account in imposing sentence.[48]

1.16 Failure to give evidence
It is irrelevant to take into account for sentencing purposes the failure of an accused person to give evidence in support of allegations made in the cross-examination of Crown witnesses.[49]

1.17 Indictment in the High Court of Justiciary
The decision of the Lord Advocate to indict a person in the High Court of Justiciary does not imply that a sentence greater than that which could be imposed in the sheriff court is necessarily warranted. The indictment of a charge in the High Court of Justiciary should not of itself influence the court in selecting an appropriate sentence.[50]

1.18 Coercion
Coercion can be a defence to a criminal charge but even where the degree of coercion is insufficient to constitute a defence it may

still mitigate a person's involvement in the offence. Where a jury returned a verdict convicting all three accused but found that two of them "were badly influenced by older persons and were easily led", one was sentenced to three years' imprisonment and the other to 30 months, the latter having been influenced by both others. The third was sentenced to 12 years' imprisonment.[51]

1.19 Political motivation
Any political or social motivation for an offence is irrelevant in relation to sentencing. Thus, a court could not take into account the argument that an offence had been committed as part of a peace demonstration.[52]

1.20 Industrial dispute
The fact that an offence was committed in the course of an industrial dispute may have an effect upon sentence. Some allowance may be made by a sentencing court in dealing with otherwise respectable citizens who commit offences in the heat engendered by a bitter industrial dispute. However, where an offender is a persistent criminal anyway, the court is entitled to deal with him as such without making any allowance for the fact that the incident occurred in the course of an industrial dispute.[53]

1.21 Breach of interdict
The fact that the commission of an offence also constitutes a breach of an interdict should not be treated as an aggravation. The two matters should be dealt with separately.[54]

1.22 Excluded sentences
A capital sentence is not competent under the 1975 Act.[55]
  No-one may be sentenced to penal servitude or to imprisonment with hard labour.[56]

1.23 Local conditions
Local conditions might play a part in determining an appropriate sentence, such as where an offender was imprisoned for a theft which, although minor, had occurred in a house that had been left unlocked, as was the custom of the country area.[57]

Notes

1. *H.M. Advocate* v. *McKenzie* 1990 J.C. 62; 1989 S.C.C.R. 587; 1990 S.L.T. 28.
2. *Addison* v. *MacKinnon* 1983 S.C.C.R. 52.
3. See para. 4.9.
4. *McCandless* v. *MacDougall* 1987 S.C.C.R. 206.
5. *Gibson* v. *Annan* 1990 S.C.C.R. 519.
6. *Curran* v. *Jessop* 1991 S.C.C.R. 150.
7. *Davidson and Anr* v. *H.M. Advocate* 1981 S.C.C.R. 371.
8. *Lambert* v. *Tudhope* 1982 S.C.C.R. 144.
9. *Brodie* v. *H.M. Advocate* 1982 S.C.C.R. 243.
10. *Donnelly* v. *MacKinnon* 1985 S.C.C.R. 391. For a further example, see *Bates* v. *H.M. Advocate* 1989 S.C.C.R. 338; 1989 S.L.T. 701.
11. *Skilling* v. *McLeod* 1987 S.C.C.R. 245.
12. *Allan* v. *H.M. Advocate* 1990 S.C.C.R. 226.
13. *Lam* v. *H.M. Advocate* 1988 S.C.C.R. 347.
14. *Smith* v. *H.M. Advocate* 1990 S.C.C.R. 251.
15. *Forrest* v. *H.M. Advocate* 1988 S.C.C.R. 481.
16. Criminal Procedure (Scotland) Act 1975, hereinafter referred to as the "1975 Act", s. 20.
17. *Campbell* v. *Johnston* 1981 S.C.C.R. 179.
18. *Paterson* v. *MacNeill* 1982 S.C.C.R. 141.
19. *Blues* v. *MacPhail* 1982 S.C.C.R. 247 at 248.
20. *McCreadie* v. *Walkingshaw* 1990 S.C.C.R. 761.
21. *Norman* v. *Smith* 1983 S.C.C.R. 100.
22. *Ruddy* v. *Wilson* 1988 S.C.C.R. 193.
23. 1975 Act, s. 430(3), which relates to summary proceedings.
24. *Seaton* v. *Allan* 1973 J.C. 24; 1974 S.L.T. 234.
25. *Caringi* v. *H.M. Advocate* 1989 S.C.C.R. 223; 1989 S.L.T. 714 (bench of five judges).
26. *McLauchlan* v. *Davidson* 1921 J.C. 45.
27. *Maguiness* v. *MacDonald* 1953 J.C. 31.
28. *Wann* v. *Macmillan* 1957 J.C. 20; 1956 S.L.T. 369.
29. *Hamilton* v. *H.M. Advocate* 1991 S.C.C.R. 282.
30. *Strawthorn* v. *McLeod* 1987 S.C.C.R. 413. Contrast the English position of allowing a discount: *R.* v. *Williams* [1983] Crim. L.R. 693. See also *Campbell* v. *H.M. Advocate* 1986 S.C.C.R. 403 in relation to backdating.
31. *Khaliq* v. *H.M. Advocate* 1984 S.C.C.R. 212.
32. *H.M. Advocate* v. *McKenzie* 1990 J.C. 62; 1989 S.C.C.R. 587; 1990 S.L.T. 28. See R. I. Wilson, "The Victim in the Criminal Justice System", 1990 S.L.T. 8.
33. *H.M. Advocate* v. *McKenzie* 1990 J.C. 62; 1989 S.C.C.R. 587; 1990 S.L.T. 28.
34. 1975 Act, ss. 216 and 428 as amended by the Criminal Justice (Scotland) Act 1987, s. 64. *cf.* D. Kelly, "Aiding and Abetting", 1988 S.L.T. 201.
35. *Simpkins* v. *H.M. Advocate* 1985 S.C.C.R. 30.
36. *Rowley* v. *H.M. Advocate* 1983 S.C.C.R. 413.
37. *Baird* v. *Lockhart* 1986 S.C.C.R. 514.
38. *Montgomery* v. *H.M. Advocate* 1987 S.C.C.R. 264. See also *Garner* v. *Lockhart* 1990 S.C.C.R. 385. For observations on a sentence imposed in respect of a failure to appear for trial on indictment, see *Beagles* v. *H.M. Advocate* 1992 S.C.C.R. 539.
39. *Kelso* v. *Crowe* 1992 S.C.C.R. 415; *Whyte* v. *Normand* 1988 S.C.C.R. 465. See further para. 4.13.
40. 1975 Act, ss. 170 and 369.

41. *Cairns* v. *H.M. Advocate* (1973) S.C.C.R. Supp. 44.
42. Children and Young Persons (Scotland) Act 1937, ss. 57(3) (as amended by the 1975 Act, Sch. 9, para. 7) and 58A (as inserted by the Social Work (Scotland) Act 1968, Sch. 2, para. 16 and amended by the 1975 Act, Sch. 9, para. 8); 1975 Act, ss. 206 (as substituted by the Criminal Justice (Scotland) Act 1980, s. 44) and 413.
43. *Cairns* v. *H.M. Advocate* (1973) S.C.C.R. Supp. 44, 48.
44. *Clayton, Petitioner* 1991 S.C.C.R. 261 at 263. See also para. 4.13.9.
45. 1975 Act, s. 429.
46. *Miller* v. *H.M. Advocate* 1985 S.C.C.R. 314.
47. *Nicolson* v. *Skeen* (1974) S.C.C.R. Supp. 74.
48. *Cooper* v. *H.M. Advocate* 1982 S.C.C.R. 87.
49. *Dorrens* v. *H.M. Advocate* 1983 S.C.C.R. 407.
50. *Khaliq* v. *H.M. Advocate* 1984 S.C.C.R. 212.
51. *H.M. Advocate* v. *Docherty* (1976) S.C.C.R. Supp. 146.
52. *Donaghy* v. *Tudhope* 1985 S.C.C.R. 118.
53. *Tait* v. *Allan* 1984 S.C.C.R. 385.
54. *Friend* v. *Normand* 1988 S.C.C.R. 232.
55. 1975 Act, s. 220. See also para. 5.4.
56. 1975 Act, s. 221.
57. *MacInnes* v. *McClory* 1991 S.C.C.R. 804.

CHAPTER 2

SENTENCING PROCEDURE

2.1 Motion for sentence

In solemn cases the prosecutor should indicate whether he is moving for sentence after an accused person has pled guilty to or been found guilty of an offence. There are no specific words which need be used. It may be that the prosecutor's actions, such as in laying previous convictions before the court, will amount to an invitation to the court to proceed to sentence, but the proper course is for the prosecutor to make an explicit, formal motion.[1] In summary proceedings it is not normal for a motion for sentence to be made.[2] It is therefore open to the prosecutor to opt not to move for sentence in respect of the indictment or complaint or in respect of certain charges in them.

2.2 Notice of penalty

In a summary case involving statutory offences a notice of penalty must be served on the accused person.[3] Unless a notice setting out an adequate penalty has been served, no penalty may be imposed in respect of a statutory offence in summary proceedings.[4] If the notice of penalty has been served on the accused person but the prosecutor is unable to place a contemporaneous copy of it before the court, a later copy may be supplied provided it is true and accurate.[5] At any time prior to the determination of the prosecution, unless just cause to the contrary is shown, the notice of penalty may be amended.[6]

An accused person may be cited to a diet if the citation is delivered personally.[7] Any complaint, warrant or other proceeding may be served by an officer of law and that service may be proved by that officer's oath or written execution.[8] The complaint and accompanying notices may alternatively be sent by recorded delivery post to the house of the accused.[9] Service of the notice of penalty is sufficiently established if the accused admits its receipt.[10] If the accused denies its receipt, the Crown will require to establish that the notice of penalty was served on him.[11] Where the accused is in custody, the notice of penalty must be served on him personally and not handed to his solicitor in his presence.[12]

If a notice of penalty is served but the accused is convicted of an offence with lesser penalties, the Crown has fulfilled its obligation to give the offender notice of the maximum penalties to which he was liable.[13] Similarly, if a notice of penalties has been served and the penalties are identical, the accused has effectively received due notice of the penalties and has suffered no prejudice. The Crown should move to amend the notice and the court should allow that motion.[14]

2.3 Previous convictions

If the Crown desires to place before the court any previous conviction to be taken into account at the time of sentencing, it must serve notice of the conviction along with the indictment or complaint. In solemn proceedings the conviction is held to apply to the accused unless he objects in writing to it at least five clear days before the trial diet; two days' notice is required in the case of a plea of guilty at a diet. In summary cases, where a plea of guilty is tendered in writing the accused is deemed to admit any previous conviction in the notice unless he expressly denies it in the written plea; in any other case the judge or the clerk of court must ask the accused whether he admits the previous conviction.[15]

The list of previous convictions may be amended to cure any errors or defects. No such amendment may be made to the prejudice of the accused.[16] The previous conviction must be dated prior to the offence charged[17] and should not be libelled if under appeal.[18] The court may also take account of convictions mentioned in a social enquiry report[19] or, in road traffic cases, endorsed on the accused's driving licence.[20] It should not consider the details of the previous offence.[21]

2.4 Interruption of proceedings

On conviction of an accused person, without adjourning the proceedings, a court may interrupt them to consider another conviction pending before that court and pass sentence in respect of it. The sentences in respect of the interrupted proceedings and the other conviction may be passed at the same time.[22]

2.5 Plea in mitigation

Prior to the imposition of sentence, the offender or his legal representative must be given the opportunity to address the court in mitigation.[23] After tendering a plea of guilty, if an accused denies an essential element of the prosecution's narrative of the facts, he should seek to withdraw the plea.[24] Evidence would not normally be led unless there was a significant dispute about mitigating factors.[25]

2.6 Adjournment and remand

2.6.1 Adjournment of case before sentence. Courts have the power, after a person has been convicted or the court has found that he committed the offence and before he has been sentenced or otherwise dealt with, to adjourn the case for the purpose of enabling enquiries to be made or of determining the most suitable method of dealing with the case. The court may remand the accused person in custody or on bail or ordain him to appear at the adjourned diet. However, a court may not so adjourn the hearing of a case for any single period exceeding three weeks.[26] A court should not defer sentence on an offender for the purpose of obtaining reports as a means of getting round the three-week period, there being a distinction to be drawn between "adjourning" for reports and "deferring sentence".[27]

The normal practice when adjourning a case in order to obtain a social enquiry or community service report should be to admit the convicted person to bail unless there are good reasons for remanding him in custody. Where the person has never been in prison before or where the court has to be satisfied after considering reports that a custodial sentence is the only appropriate disposal, very good reasons would be required in order to justify a refusal of bail while reports are being obtained.[28]

An accused person who is remanded may appeal against the refusal of bail or against the conditions imposed within 24 hours of his remand by note of appeal presented to the High Court of Justiciary. The High Court of Justiciary, in court or in chambers, may after hearing parties, either review the order appealed against or confirm it. If it reviews it, it may either grant bail on such conditions as it thinks fit or ordain the accused to appear at the adjourned diet.[29]

A review of a court's decision under s. 30 of the 1975 Act has no application to bail at this stage.[30] If the accused does not appeal within 24 hours he cannot fall back on the review provisions of s. 30.

2.6.2 Social enquiry report. A sheriff in his report to the High Court of Justiciary indicated that he was unable to place as much weight on the social enquiry report that was provided as he would have liked in view of the directive issued by the director of social work in that region (Fife) that no reporter could ever recommend that a custodial sentence be imposed on any person appearing before a court. The appeal court agreed that the inevitable consequence of such a directive must be that less importance would be attached to social enquiry reports than otherwise would be the case.[31]

2.6.3 Remand for enquiry into physical or mental condition. Where a person is charged before a court with an offence punishable with imprisonment and the court is satisfied that he did the act or made the omission charged but is of the opinion that an enquiry ought to be made into his physical or mental condition before the method of dealing with him is determined, the court should remand him in custody or on bail to enable a medical examination and report to be made. No single period of remand may exceed three weeks.[32]

Where a person is so remanded on bail, one of the conditions of granting bail should be that he shall undergo a medical examination by a duly qualified medical practitioner or, where the enquiry is into his medical condition and the bail order so specifies, two such practitioners. There should be a further condition that the accused shall attend at an institution or place or on any such practitioner specified in the bail order and, where the enquiry is into his mental condition, comply with any directions which may be given to him in this regard by anyone so specified or by any class of person so specified.[33]

There may be a further bail condition that the person shall, for the purpose of the examination, reside in an institution or place so specified, not being an institution or place to which he could have been remanded in custody, until the expiry of any specified period or until he is discharged therefrom, whichever first occurs.[34]

If the court remands the person in custody, it must send to the institution or place in which he is to be detained a statement of the reasons why it is of the view that an enquiry ought to be made into his physical or mental condition. Any information before the court about his physical or mental condition should be included. If the court releases the person on bail, it should send a similar statement to the institution or place at which or to the person by whom the accused is to be examined.[35]

There is a similar right of appeal against the refusal of bail as where the court adjourns a case before sentence.[36]

A party applying for a medical examination to be made must in general put forward sufficient material to enable the court to form an opinion that enquiry ought to be made. It is the duty of his advisers to make some investigation of the circumstances surrounding the offence and of the person's physical and mental condition in order to give reasons in support of the application.[37]

2.7 Form of sentence

A sentence in a solemn case should be announced in open court by the judge and entered in the record. It is not necessary to read the entry of the sentence from the record.[38] A sentence imposed by a summary court should, unless otherwise provided, be pronounced in open court in the presence of the accused.[39]

2.8 Modification of sentence

In summary proceedings it is competent to alter or modify a sentence at any time before a sentence of imprisonment has been commenced. No higher sentence than that originally pronounced may be imposed.[40] The accused need not be present.[41]

An erroneously recorded or incomplete extract of a sentence passed or court order made may be corrected by the clerk of court. After the sentence or order is executed the authority of the court is required. If the case is appealed and the proceedings have been transmitted to the Clerk of Justiciary, the authority of the High Court of Justiciary is required.[42] In the latter two cases the correction must be intimated to the prosecutor and to the offender or his solicitor.[43]

2.9 Same judge

If a judge places an offender on deferred sentence, when the offender reappears on the expiry of the period of deferment, he should be dealt with by the same judge unless the exigencies of business demand that that should not be the case. Where a different sheriff dealt with a case on the termination of the period of deferment and imposed a custodial sentence, the Court of Criminal Appeal quashed it and imposed a fine instead since it appeared to the court that the original sheriff, having called on the accused to make substantial amends which he had made, would not have imposed a custodial sentence.[44]

For reasons of fairness and consistency, so far as practicable the sentencing process should be continued by the same judge until the case has been finally concluded. However, if a judge has simply continued a case for reports, the sentencing process has not yet begun. The diet has simply been adjourned; sentence has not been deferred. In this situation, it would not be necessary for the original judge to determine sentence and, if there were more than one complaint or indictment, all outstanding charges should be considered together by one judge.[45]

2.10 Offender abroad

If an offender pleads guilty to an offence such as driving with an excess of alcohol or driving dangerously and is abroad for some time when sentence is to be passed, it may be unreasonable to insist on his personal appearance.[46] However, that has the consequence that a sentence of imprisonment could not be imposed since it could not be imposed in his absence.

2.11 Mitigation of penalties

In accordance with the wide discretion given to courts to determine sentence, even where a penalty has been fixed by statute a lower sentence may be imposed. The courts have powers in proceedings in respect of the contravention of any statute or order, where such contravention involves imprisonment, the imposition of a fine, or the finding of caution for good behaviour:

(1) to reduce the period of imprisonment;
(2) in solemn proceedings, to substitute for imprisonment a fine;
(3) in summary proceedings, to substitute for imprisonment a fine not exceeding the prescribed sum in the case of an offence triable either summarily or on indictment and not exceeding level 4 on the standard scale in the case of an offence triable only summarily;
(4) in solemn proceedings, to substitute the finding of caution not exceeding the prescribed sum and the period of 12 months for a fine or imprisonment;
(5) in summary proceedings, to substitute the finding of caution for a fine or imprisonment;
(6) to reduce the amount of any fine; and
(7) to dispense with the finding of caution.

However, where any Act carries into effect a treaty, convention or agreement with a foreign state which stipulates for a fine of a minimum amount, that amount may not be reduced. The power to mitigate does not apply to proceedings taken under any Act relating to the armed services.[47]

Where a statute fixes a minimum penalty, it has been held competent under previous legislation to modify the penalty still further.[48]

Notes

1. *Noon* v. *H.M. Advocate* 1960 J.C. 52; 1960 S.L.T. (Notes) 51.
2. See *Skeen* v. *Sullivan* 1980 S.L.T. (Notes) 11 although in that case a motion for sentence was made but the question arose as to the need for a prosecutor's motion when the accused subsequently failed to appear.
3. 1975 Act, s. 311(5). However, see the Road Traffic Offenders Act 1988, ss. 31(2), 32(6) and 60(6) for exclusions.
4. *Scott* v. *Annan* 1981 S.C.C.R. 172; 1982 S.L.T. 90.
5. *Smith* v. *Moffat* 1981 S.C.C.R. 291 (Sh. Ct.).
6. 1975 Act, s. 335(1).
7. 1975 Act, s. 316(2).
8. 1975 Act, s. 326; *Muir* v. *Carmichael* 1988 S.C.C.R. 79.
9. 1975 Act, s. 316(3).
10. *Aitchison* v. *Wringe* 1985 S.C.C.R. 134; 1985 S.L.T. 449.
11. *Cowan* v. *Guild* 1991 S.C.C.R. 424; 1992 S.L.T. 939.

12. *Geddes* v. *Hamilton* 1986 J.C. 60; 1986 S.C.C.R. 165; 1986 S.L.T. 536.

13. *Cardle* v. *Campbell* 1985 S.C.C.R. 309.

14. *Donnachie* v. *Smith* 1989 S.C.C.R. 144; *Fletcher* v. *Webster* 1991 S.L.T. 256.

15. 1975 Act, ss. 68 and 357 as amended by the Criminal Justice (Scotland) Act 1980, hereinafter referred to as the "1980 Act", Schs. 4, 6 and 8 and s. 40 respectively. See also 1975 Act, ss. 159–164, 356 and 358. On proof of service of the schedule of previous convictions, see *Cowan* v. *Guild* 1991 S.C.C.R. 424; 1992 S.L.T. 939. On taking account of previous convictions brought to the attention of the court, see *Henderson* v. *Heywood* 1992 S.C.C.R. 610.

16. 1975 Act, ss. 161(2) and 335(1).

17. *H.M. Advocate* v. *Graham* (1842) 1 Broun 445.

18. *McCall* v.*Mitchell* 1911 S.C.(J.) 1; 6 Adam 303.

19. *Sharp* v. *Stevenson* 1948 S.L.T. (Notes) 79; *Sillars* v. *Copeland* 1966 J.C. 8; 1966 S.L.T. 89.

20. Road Traffic Offenders Act 1988, s. 31(1).

21. *Connell* v. *Mitchell* 1909 S.C.(J.) 13; 5 Adam 641; *Baker* v. *M'Fadyean* 1952 S.L.T. (Notes) 69.

22. Act of Adjournal (Consolidation) 1988, rules 74 and 123.

23. *Graham* v. *McLennan* 1911 S.C.(J.) 16; 6 Adam 315; *Ewart* v. *Strathern* 1924 J.C. 45; 1924 S.L.T. 359; *Falconer* v. *Jessop* 1975 S.L.T. (Notes) 78 ; *Martin* v. *Crowe* 1992 S.C.C.R. 388; *Bassi* v. *Normand* 1992 S.C.C.R. 413; 1992 S.L.T. 341. *Cf. Stewart* v. *Lowe* 1991 S.C.C.R. 317 on convicting without first hearing the defence agent.

24. Renton and Brown's *Criminal Procedure* (5th edn.) para. 15–11.

25. *Galloway* v. *Adair* 1947 J.C. 7; 1947 S.L.T. 23; *Forbes* v. *H.M. Advocate* 1963 J.C. 68; *Barn* v. *Smith* 1978 J.C. 17; 1978 S.L.T. (Notes) 3; Renton and Brown's *Criminal Procedure* (5th edn.) para. 10–71.

26. 1975 Act, ss. 179(1) and 380(1) as amended by the Bail etc. (Scotland) Act 1980, s. 5 and the 1980 Act, s. 83(2), Sch. 7, paras. 36 and 59.

27. *H.M. Advocate* v. *Clegg* 1990 J.C. 318; 1990 S.C.C.R. 293; 1991 S.L.T. 192; *Wilson* v. *Donald* 1992 S.C.C.R. 654.

28. *Smith* v. *McC.* 1982 J.C. 67; 1982 S.C.C.R. 115; 1982 S.L.T. 421 (sub nom. *Smith* v. *M.*); *McGoldrick* v. *Normand* 1988 S.C.C.R. 83; 1988 S.L.T. 273.

29. 1975 Act, ss. 179(2) and 380(2) as added by the Bail etc. (Scotland) Act 1980, s. 5 and amended by the 1980 Act, Sch. 7 paras. 36 and 59.

30. *Long* v. *H.M. Advocate* 1984 S.C.C.R. 161.

31. *Bellamy* v. *H.M. Advocate* 1987 S.C.C.R. 101.

32. 1975 Act, ss. 180(1) and 381(1).

33. 1975 Act, ss. 180(2) and 381(2) as amended by the Bail etc. (Scotland) Act 1980, Sch. 1 paras. 5 and 9.

34. *Ibid.*

35. 1975 Act, ss. 180(4) and 381(4).

36. 1975 Act, ss. 180(5) and 381(5) as added by the Bail etc. (Scotland) Act 1980, s. 6.

37. *H.M. Advocate* v. *Scobie* 1952 J.C. 96.

38. 1975 Act, s. 217.

39. 1975 Act, s. 433. For the appropriate form of record of a sentence in summary proceedings, see 1975 Act, s. 430(1).

40. 1975 Act, s. 434(1). See also *Patrick* v. *Copeland* 1969 J.C. 42; 1970 S.L.T. 71.

41. 1975 Act, s. 434(3) as amended by 1980 Act, Sch. 8.

42. 1975 Act, ss. 227A(1) and (2), 439(1) and (2) as inserted by 1980 Act, ss. 20 and 54.

43. 1975 Act, ss. 227A(3) and 439(3).

44. *Islam* v. *H.M. Advocate* 1989 S.C.C.R. 109. See also *Main* v. *Jessop* 1989 S.C.C.R. 437.
45. *Beattie* v. *McGlennan* 1990 S.C.C.R. 497; 1991 S.L.T. 384; *Thomson* v. *Smith* 1982 J.C. 40; 1982 S.C.C.R. 57; 1982 S.L.T. 546.
46. *Imrie* v. *McGlennan* 1990 S.C.C.R. 218.
47. 1975 Act, ss. 193 (as amended by the 1980 Act, ss. 46(2), 83(3) and Sch. 8) and 394 (as amended by the Criminal Law Act 1977, ss. 46(2), 63(1), Sch. 6 para. 1, Sch. 8, Sch. 11 para. 7 and the Criminal Justice Act 1982, ss. 56, Sch. 7 para. 10).
48. *Lambie* v. *Mearns* (1903) 4 Adam 207. See also *Paton* v. *Neilson* (1903) 4 Adam 268 and *McDonald* v. *Wood and Bruce Ltd.* 1950 J.C. 72; 1950 S.L.T. 287.

CHAPTER 3

APPEAL AGAINST SENTENCE

3.1 General

Any person convicted of an offence, apart from one for which the sentence is fixed by law, may appeal against the sentence imposed. As well as an appeal against conviction, appeal may be taken against conviction and sentence or against sentence alone. The appeal is to the Court of Criminal Appeal. The ground for review is that of a miscarriage of justice, including one relating to additional evidence not reasonably available at the trial.[1]

An appeal against sentence alone in solemn cases is initiated by lodging a note of appeal with the Clerk of Justiciary within two weeks of the sentence being passed.[2] Where sentence is deferred, proceedings are deemed to be finally determined for appeal purposes on the day on which sentence is first so deferred.[3] A note of the grounds of appeal must be given and, except by leave of the High Court of Justiciary on cause shown, it is not possible to found on a ground not contained in the note of appeal.[4]

In summary cases appeal against sentence alone is also by note of appeal. However, an appeal based on a fundamental irregularity would be brought by bill of suspension.[5] The note of appeal must be lodged with the clerk of court from which the appeal is to be taken within one week of the passing of the sentence.[6] It must state the ground of appeal[7] and should specify why the sentence is considered excessive or inappropriate.[8] It may also crave for bail or for suspension of an order such as disqualification.

If the prosecutor wishes to challenge the competency of any sentence imposed he must do so by stated case.

If an accused person appeals against conviction or sentence, the court may suspend any disqualification, forfeiture or disability ordered pending the determination of the appeal.[9] However, the court has no power to suspend a community service order pending appeal.[10]

23

3.2   Function of the Court of Criminal Appeal

The function of the Court of Criminal Appeal in an appeal against sentence is not to consider as a court of review whether or not it is of the opinion that some form of sentence other than that passed by the judge in the court below should be imposed. Its function is to decide whether in all the circumstances the sentence imposed by the original judge was or was not excessive. It is only if it was excessive that the appeal court is called upon to determine what the appropriate sentence should be.[11]

The Court of Criminal Appeal has declared itself slow to interfere with a decision of a trial judge, who has had many benefits which are denied to it. The main advantage of the judge presiding at the trial would be that the background circumstances against which the offence was committed would normally have been disclosed in the evidence. The trial judge would also have had the advantage of seeing and possibly hearing the offender in court and of forming his own impression of the type of person with whom he was dealing. This might have been a contrary impression to that expressed by the social worker in the social enquiry report.[12]

3.3   Change in circumstances prior to hearing of appeal

The Court of Criminal Appeal has taken account of changes in an offender's circumstances between the imposition of a sentence and the hearing of the appeal. Where an offender had between interim liberation and the date of the appeal reconciled with his family and obtained employment, the appeal court took cognizance of this intervening marked improvement and quashed a prison sentence which had earlier been imposed, choosing instead to defer sentence.[13]

Where, due to a change in the offender's circumstances between the imposition of sentence and the hearing of the appeal, another method of disposing of the case apart from a custodial sentence had presented itself, the appeal court has on occasion adopted that other option.[14] In one case where an unemployed person who had been sentenced to 60 days' imprisonment for a second offence of driving with excess alcohol had obtained employment at an annual salary of £10,000 by the date of his appeal, the sentence of imprisonment was quashed and a fine of £1,000 imposed.[15] This has given rise to questions as to whether the role being exercised by the Court of Criminal Appeal was that of a court of appeal or of review.[16]

3.4 Hearing of appeal

An appellant in a summary case who has been granted bail must appear personally in court at the hearing of the appeal or it will be deemed to be abandoned unless there is cause shown for the appeal to be heard in his absence.[17] In solemn cases the accused would normally be on bail or brought from prison but the High Court of Justiciary may deal with an appeal and sentence him in his absence.[18]

3.5 Disposal of appeal

The Court of Criminal Appeal may dispose of an appeal against sentence by affirming the sentence. Alternatively, if the appeal court considers that, having regard to all of the circumstances, a different sentence should have been passed, it may dispose of an appeal against sentence by quashing the sentence and passing another sentence in substitution for it. That sentence may be more or less severe than the original one.[19] In summary cases the appeal court may not increase the sentence beyond the maximum sentence which could have been passed by the inferior court.[20] In summary cases the Court of Criminal Appeal has power to award such expenses both in the High Court of Justiciary and in the inferior court as it may think fit in an appeal by note of appeal.[21] Expenses may also be awarded in summary cases where a conviction or conviction and sentence are set aside with the consent of the prosecutor, subject to a maximum amount.[22]

3.6 Increase of sentence

Although the Court of Criminal Appeal does have the power to increase a sentence appealed against, that power is exercised sparingly. There are instances where it has been used in recent years.

Sentences of six years' imprisonment have been increased to 10 years. Two offenders who pled guilty to possessing 507 counterfeit £20 notes and a sawn-off shotgun were sentenced to three years' imprisonment on each charge, the sentences to run consecutively. As the appeal developed, counsel for one of the appellants moved the court to allow his appeal to be abandoned but that request was refused. The appeal court regarded the offences as very serious and the original sentences as inadequate. It quashed the sentences and substituted consecutive sentences of five years' imprisonment on each charge.[23]

In one case the sentences were increased but the end result remained the same. Sentences of one year's imprisonment on two charges, to run consecutively, were quashed and the sentences were increased to two years' imprisonment on each charge, the sentences to run concurrently.[24]

A sentence of 18 months' detention for possession of a C.S. gas canister at a football match has been increased to two years.[25] A fine for a fifth speeding offence has been increased from £20 to £400.[26] A £250 fine for assaulting a water bailiff has been increased to £500.[27] A sentence of 12 months' detention imposed on a 17-year-old convicted of assaulting a stranger in a street by striking him on the head with a wooden stave and stamping on his head has been increased to one of two years' detention.[28]

Sentences in respect of breach of bail have been made to run consecutively to other sentences where no reason had been shown for making them concurrent.[29]

Notes

1. 1975 Act, ss. 228 and 442 as substituted by the 1980 Act, Sch. 2 para. 1, Sch. 3 para. 1, Sch. 6 paras. 6 and 7.
2. 1975 Act, s. 233(1). (S. 233 was substituted by the 1980 Act, Sch. 2 para. 5.)
3. 1975 Act, s. 231(4) as substituted by the 1980 Act, Sch. 2 para. 3, Sch. 6 para. 6.
4. 1975 Act, s. 233(2) and (3).
5. 1975 Act, s. 442B, as added by the 1980 Act, s. 34, Sch. 3 para. 1, Sch. 6 para. 7.
6. 1975 Act, s. 453B(1) and (2) as added by the 1980 Act, s. 34, Sch. 3 para. 13, Sch. 6 para. 7. The position in respect of deferred sentence is the same as in solemn proceedings: 1975 Act, s. 451(3) as substituted by the 1980 Act, Sch. 3 para. 10, Sch. 6 para. 7.
7. 1975 Act, s. 453B(1). The timetable to be observed thereafter is also set out in this section, as is the means of abandoning an appeal and the appointment of an expert assessor.
8. High Court of Justiciary Practice Note, 29 March 1985, 1985 S.L.T. 120.
9. 1975 Act, ss. 264(3), 443A, as added by the Criminal Justice (Scotland) Act 1987, s. 68.

10. *Farmer* v. *Guild* 1992 S.L.T. 320.
11. *Donaldson* v. *H.M. Advocate* 1983 S.C.C.R. 216.
12. *Addison* v. *MacKinnon* 1983 S.C.C.R. 52.
13. *Rennie* v. *MacNeill* 1984 S.C.C.R. 11.
14. *Logan* v. *Douglas* 1986 S.C.C.R. 590.
15. *McLean* v. *MacDougall* 1989 S.C.C.R. 625.
16. See the Commentary to *McLean* v. *MacDougall* 1989 S.C.C.R. 625.
17. 1975 Act, s. 453E, as added by the 1980 Act, s. 34, Sch. 3 para. 13, Sch. 6 para. 7; *Manson, Petitioner* 1991 S.L.T. 96.
18. 1975 Act, s. 258.
19. 1975 Act, ss. 254(3) (as substituted by the 1980 Act, s. 33, Sch. 2 para. 18, Sch. 6 para. 6) and 453C (as added by the 1980 Act, s. 34, Sch. 3 para. 13, Sch. 6 para. 7).
20. 1975 Act, s. 453C(1)(b).
21. 1975 Act, s. 453C(2), as inserted by the 1980 Act, Sch.3. Expenses are not awarded in solemn cases: 1975 Act, s. 266.
22. 1975 Act, s. 453, as amended by the 1980 Act s. 46 and Sch. 3 and S.I. 1991 810; *Hamilton* v. *Friel* 1992 S.C.C.R. 67; 1992 S.L.T. 819.
23. *Grant* v. *H.M. Advocate* 1985 S.C.C.R. 431.
24. *Walker* v. *H.M. Advocate* 1987 S.C.C.R. 379.
25. *Donnelly* v. *H.M. Advocate* 1988 S.C.C.R. 386.
26. *Briggs* v. *Guild* 1987 S.C.C.R. 141.
27. *Mays* v. *Brown* 1988 S.C.C.R. 549.
28. *Smeaton* v. *H.M. Advocate* 1992 S.C.C.R. 587.
29. *Kelso* v. *Crowe* 1992 S.C.C.R. 415.

CHAPTER 4

CUSTODY

4.1 Imprisonment

No person may now be sentenced to penal servitude or to imprisonment with hard labour and every Act conferring power on a court to pass such a sentence is to be construed as conferring a power to impose imprisonment.[1] Accordingly, the only form of custodial sentence for those aged 21 or over is imprisonment.

4.2 Detention of young offenders

Imprisonment may not be imposed on a person under 21 years of age.[2] A court may impose detention on a person who is not less than 16 but under 21 years of age where it would have power to impose imprisonment on an adult. The period of detention may not exceed the maximum period of imprisonment which might otherwise have been imposed.[3] The detention is in a young offenders institution.[4]

Detention may not be imposed unless the court is of the opinion that no other method of dealing with the offender is appropriate. The court must state its reasons for that opinion and, except in the High Court of Justiciary, those reasons must be entered in the record of proceedings. Merely recording "in view of previous record" without first stating "being of opinion that no other method of dealing with the offender was appropriate" would be insufficient.[5] The Court of Criminal Appeal has highlighted the importance of sheriffs and justices complying with these provisions.[6] To enable the court to form an opinion, it must obtain a report on the offender's circumstances and it must also take into account any information before it concerning the offender's character and physical and mental condition.[7]

In considering whether there is any other appropriate method of dealing with an offender, if a court considers that a fine would be an appropriate penalty for the offence it should not reject a fine on the basis that the offender would have insufficient means to meet it.[8]

4.3 Detention of children

A person under 16 years of age will normally be dealt with by a children's hearing. If such a person is prosecuted in the High Court of Justiciary or the sheriff court, the court may refer the case to a children's hearing and must do so if the child is under supervision.[9]

Where a child is convicted in solemn proceedings of any offence other than murder and the court is of the opinion that no other method of dealing with him is appropriate, it may sentence him to be detained for a specified period. The child will be detained in such place as the Secretary of State may direct.[10] The Secretary of State may release a person so detained on specified conditions.[11] It is competent to order that a child be detained without limit of time in other cases as well as those of murder.[12]

A person who has been sentenced as a child to be detained for over 18 months may be released on licence.[13] As a general rule, judges should bear in mind that it may not be appropriate to order a custodial sentence to run consecutively to a sentence of detention on a child.[14]

Where a child appears before a sheriff in summary proceedings and pleads guilty to or is found guilty of an offence, the sheriff may order that he be detained in residential care by the local authority for such period not exceeding one year as the sheriff may determine. This power applies only in relation to those offences in respect of which it is competent to impose imprisonment on an adult.[15]

4.4 Powers of the High Court of Justiciary

There is no maximum limit on the power of the High Court of Justiciary in relation to common law crimes. For statutory offences, its power is limited to the penalty provided in the statute.

4.5 Maximum limits in sheriff court

On the conviction on indictment of a person, a sheriff may not pass a sentence of imprisonment for a term exceeding three years. However, this does not authorise the imposition by a sheriff of a sentence in excess of the sentence specified by an enactment as the maximum sentence which may be imposed on conviction of an offence.[16] If a person appeared on separate indictments for technical reasons only, the maximum total sentence which the sheriff could impose would be three years' imprisonment.[17]

Exercising his summary powers, a sheriff on convicting a person of a common law offence may award imprisonment for any period not exceeding three months.[18] No cumulo period may exceed the three months' overriding maximum limit. An additional sentence of imprisonment in lieu of payment of a fine which took the period beyond the statutory maximum power of the court would be incompetent, although in appropriate cases a fine could competently be imposed and recovered by civil diligence.[19] A fine in addition to the maximum period of imprisonment could be imposed if available and recovered by civil diligence.

Where a person is convicted of a second or subsequent offence inferring dishonest appropriation of property or attempt at it or a second or subsequent offence inferring personal violence, a sheriff may sentence him to imprisonment for any period not exceeding six months. The term "personal violence" has on occasion been misconstrued. No reference is made to an attempt in respect of it. The offence in question must be one from which it may be inferred that personal violence was actually used. The use of words involving threats to cause alarm or fear that personal violence may be used in the future does not imply that personal violence was used in the actual offence.[20]

A breach of the peace which involved shouting and swearing and malicious damage was wrongly taken to be personal violence and so a six month sentence was quashed and one of three months imposed.[21] Again, a sheriff wrongly took the view that previous convictions for having an offensive weapon and for reckless discharge of an air pistol inferred personal violence and imposed a sentence of six months' imprisonment which was reduced on appeal to three months' imprisonment.[22]

4.6   Remit to High Court of Justiciary for sentence

Where at any diet in sheriff solemn proceedings sentence falls to be imposed but the sheriff holds that any competent sentence which he could impose is inadequate, he should remit the convicted person to the High Court of Justiciary for an appropriate sentence. He should endorse upon the record copy of the indictment a certificate of the plea or verdict, write an interlocutor on the record copy remitting the person to the High Court of Justiciary and append to the interlocutor a note of his reasons for the remit.[23]

It is competent for a sheriff to remit a convicted person to the High Court of Justiciary for sentence where under an enactment an offence is punishable by imprisonment for a term exceeding three years but the enactment restricts the power of the sheriff to impose a sentence of imprisonment for a term exceeding three years. The High Court of Justiciary may pass any sentence which it could have passed if the person had been convicted before it.[24]

It is incompetent to remit a convicted person for sentence when the maximum penalty for the offence charged is within the competence of the sheriff. Where an offender appears on two or more indictments each must be considered by the sheriff separately and where the maximum sentence which could be imposed on one indictment is within his own competence he must himself deal with that indictment.[25] If two or more accused appear on the indictment, both or all should be remitted to the High Court of Justiciary.[26]

4.7   Maximum limit in district court

The district court is entitled on convicting of a common law offence to award imprisonment for any period not exceeding 60 days.[27] It may not try any statutory offence where the maximum penalty exceeds 60 days' imprisonment or a fine of level 4 on the standard scale.[28]

It may also award imprisonment for failure to pay a fine or to find caution, provided that in no case may the total imprisonment exceed 60 days.[29] Thus, where an offender was convicted on two charges and was sentenced to 60 days' imprisonment on one charge and fined £2 on the other, with 20 days' imprisonment in default of payment within seven days to run consecutively, the sentences were incompetent since the total imprisonment could have exceeded 60 days.[30]

4.8 Maximum sentence for offence – sub-charges

What determines the sentence which can be imposed in respect of a particular charge on an indictment is the nature of the charge. If sub-charges are relied upon to demonstrate that an offence has been committed, although a separate sentence could be imposed in respect of each sub-charge, the total sentence could not exceed the maximum for the offence. It would be different if the sub-charges had each been made the subject of a separate charge.[31]

4.9 First custodial sentence

A court may not pass a custodial sentence on a person of or over 21 years of age who has not previously received a custodial sentence in the United Kingdom unless the court considers that no other method of dealing with him is appropriate. In order to determine whether any other method of dealing with the person is appropriate, the court must obtain such information as it can from a local authority officer or otherwise about the offender's circumstances. This is generally in the form of a social enquiry report prepared by a social worker. The court must also take into account any information before it concerning the offender's character and physical and mental condition.[32]

A summary court must state the reason for its opinion that no other method of dealing with the offender is appropriate and that reason must be entered in the record of the proceedings.[33]

In all cases of children and offenders under the age of 21 years a period of detention may not be imposed unless the court is of the opinion that no other disposal is appropriate.[34]

The Court of Criminal Appeal has indicated that it is reluctant to send a person to prison for the first time, even for a grave offence. It has given an offender an opportunity of avoiding a custodial sentence for a "particularly nasty assault" by punching and kicking, causing the victim to suffer bruising and the loss of two teeth. A sentence of 60 days' imprisonment was quashed and a £500 fine with the alternative of 60 days' imprisonment in the event of non-payment imposed.[35]

The Court of Criminal Appeal has quashed a prison sentence imposed on a first offender who pled guilty to a fraud systematically persisted in for a very considerable time resulting in the obtaining of £1,961.94 in supplementary benefit payments. The offender had made false statements in claiming that she was unemployed. The appeal court considered that the question was whether the deterrent value of the sentence of 30 days' imprisonment outweighed the possible consequences of the sentence upon the offender's children who, according to the social enquiry report, would have been likely to suffer serious emotional damage as a result of the separation from their mother. Two years' probation was ordered in place of the imprisonment.[36]

The appeal court has also quashed a prison sentence on a first offender who pled guilty to indecent assault on and theft from a 16-year-old girl.[37] Imprisonment was considered to be excessive for a first offender who assaulted his wife on three occasions.[38] Two 16-year-old first offenders who pled guilty to theft by housebreaking of £15,000 of property from a department store had their sentences of nine months' detention quashed. All of the property was recovered.[39]

In a case of perjury a three months' custodial sentence on a 17-year-old first offender has been quashed and a fine of £500 substituted. The appeal court took into consideration the obtaining of employment by the appellant, his application to join the air force which a custodial sentence would have barred and his extreme youth.[40] A first offender who pled guilty to eleven offences of forcing open cars, stealing property valued at £1,000 from six of them, had a sentence of three months' detention quashed and a community service order substituted.[41]

However, the gravity of the offences committed may make a custodial disposal the only appropriate one, even for first offenders. This was the case where a group formed themselves into a team, caused £1,200 of damage, stole £371 and damaged public telephones thereby depriving the public who might have required to use them in emergencies.[42]

A sentence of six months' imprisonment for a 43-year-old female first offender who pled guilty to an indictment containing sixteen charges of shoplifting was not considered to be excessive.[43]

Where a first offender was imprisoned for three months for possession of a flick knife, the appeal court refused to interfere with the discretion of the sheriff. It was a serious offence and the sheriff's disposal, while not the one that the appeal court would have chosen, could not have been regarded as an improper use of his discretion. The appeal court was therefore not in a position to intervene and substitute its own view on what was the appropriate sentence.[44]

A custodial sentence was deemed necessary for the reset of a shotgun by a first offender, due to the gravity of the offence.[45]

A sentence of three months' imprisonment on a first offender for drinking and driving has been upheld where a man had consciously driven after consuming a considerable quantity of alcohol when his blood/alcohol level was twice the legal limit, leading him to lose control of his car with foreseeable consequences.[46]

For a planned and deliberate serious assault by first offenders which was a case of individuals taking the law into their own hands, the appeal court was quite satisfied that the only appropriate disposal was a custodial one.[47]

4.10   Life sentence

There are a number of instances where a life sentence has been imposed for a crime other than murder. Even where a sentence of life imprisonment has been imposed for the protection of the public, the sentence has been held to differ from a sentence of preventative detention which has now been removed by statute and which would accordingly be incompetent.[48]

A life sentence has been held to have been the most humane disposal available to the court and a disposal which was not inimical to the best interests of an offender who pled guilty to a "particularly horrible crime" of assault with intent to rape and attempted rape.[49] The appeal court pointed out that it was a sentence which was subject to review from time to time and which might be terminated by the grant of licence when and if it was shown that the risk of the offender's release from the point of view of the public could be seen to be small.

A sentence of life imprisonment has also been imposed on a fire raiser who was described as being highly dangerous but who was not susceptible to medical treatment.[50]

In one instance a person accused of murder pled guilty to culpable homicide due to diminished responsibility, which plea was accepted by the Crown. Nonetheless, he was sentenced to life imprisonment on the view that there could be no assurance that he would not be likely to act in a similar way in the future.[51] Again, the life sentence was considered by the appeal court as the best possible sentence from the point of view of the offender and the public. His position would be reviewed periodically and in the absence of any conduct of a violent character his release might in time be viewed as an acceptable risk.

Similarly, in a case of rape a life sentence was considered to be not only the correct but also the best sentence in the public interest and also in the interest of the appellant himself. The offender had indicated that he wished to receive any necessary treatment to control his sexual impulses, which would have involved future psychiatric assessment. The sentence would be under regular review and he could be released when his condition merited it.[52]

Even where there was no medical or psychiatric evidence before the court, a judge would be entitled to conclude that a person convicted of sexual offences with previous analogous convictions was an incorrigible sexual offender and that accordingly he was someone from whom the public required the protection of a life sentence.[53]

4.11   Minimum and short sentences

A court of summary jurisdiction may not imprison a person for a period of less than five days.[54]

Even in circumstances where a substantial custodial sentence would be warranted, a short custodial sentence may be inappropriate. A sentence of 14 days' imprisonment has been disapproved of and quashed, being a sentence which was unlikely to achieve anything. It was seen as being such a short sentence that it was unlikely to do any good either to the offender or to the prison system. A sentence of this length may be inappropriate even although had a lengthier custodial sentence been imposed it would have been difficult to have said that it was excessive.[55]

The Court of Criminal Appeal has quashed a sentence of 21 days' detention on the basis that it would have done no particular good to the offender, would have been of little value to the institution in which he would have had to serve it and it might have resulted in the offender losing the chance of training for employment and of employment itself for all time.[56]

However, the appeal court refused to interfere with sentences of 30 days' detention imposed as a "short, sharp shock" on three 16 year olds, with no or little previous convictions, who were convicted of assault.[57]

4.12   Detention in the precincts of courts

If a summary court would be empowered to impose imprisonment or detention on an offender it may instead of so doing order that he be detained in the precincts of the court or at any police station until such hour as the court may direct. That hour may not be later than 8 p.m. on the day on which he is convicted.[58]

4.13   Consecutive sentences

4.13.1   General. A sentence following on a conviction by a court may be framed so as to take effect on the expiry of any previous sentence which at the date of such conviction the accused is undergoing.[59]

4.13.2   Exceeding individual maximum limits. If the court imposes consecutive sentences on different charges in the one complaint it must do so within its overall limit in respect of an individual charge.[60]

In an earlier case Lord Justice-Clerk Grant held that a court did have power to impose a consecutive sentence although the total resulting sentence would be in excess of the maximum individual limit of the court.[61] Where there was more than one indictment, he stated that the indictments were to be regarded as being wholly separate, requiring to be called separately, dealt with separately, disposed of separately and sentenced upon separately. There was therefore no reason why on the second indictment a sheriff should not pass a sentence consecutive to that imposed in the first which together would amount to over two years' imprisonment, the maximum limit at that time for a sheriff in solemn cases. At the same time, the presiding judge should take into account the sentence which he might have passed had all of the charges been taken on one indictment.

This case was not followed by the Court of Criminal Appeal in *Williamson* v. *Farrell* in relation to two complaints, one of which concerned disqualified driving on the same occasion as the charges on the first complaint and which would have been on the same complaint but for this.[62] Since then, if the charges could all have been included in one complaint or indictment but were separated for technical reasons only, the sentences have been limited to those within the total powers of the court.

Thus, someone who drives at the same time with an excess of alcohol and while disqualified and appears on separate complaints should not receive more than the maximum available on one complaint.[63] In a solemn case a consecutive sentence for a separate indictment relating to driving while disqualified was quashed since along with a related indictment it would have exceeded the three years maximum total sentence which the sheriff could impose. A consecutive sentence of six months' imprisonment was imposed in its place, which kept the sentence within the sheriff's sentencing powers while still imposing a sentence for driving while disqualified.[64] Sentences imposed on separate complaints on charges of driving recklessly and while disqualified, though they relate to the same incident, may be made consecutive to each other provided the total sentence does not exceed the maximum which could have been imposed had both charges been on the same complaint.[65]

It is now clear that it is competent to impose consecutive sentences on separate complaints dealt with on the same day even if the sentences total more than could have been imposed on one complaint.[66] The statutory limitations merely enact that the effective sentence on one complaint must not exceed those limits.

Although competent, whether a court is entitled to impose consecutive sentences on separate complaints exceeding the individual limit will depend upon whether or not the various complaints before the court should in all equity be treated as one. Such factors as the possibility and reasonable practicability and fairness of incorporating all the charges in one complaint or dealing with all complaints at one time can legitimately be taken into account in deciding whether the interests of justice call for the complaints to be treated as one. The test is one of fairness, which includes fairness to the accused and to the public interest.[67]

A consecutive sentence on numerous complaints amounting to 12 months' imprisonment has been upheld by the Court of

Criminal Appeal, indicating that it would have allowed a greater total sentence, the sheriff having "acted indulgently" towards the offender.[68]

Where an offender appeared in court on one complaint inter alia for attempted housebreaking and later appeared on another complaint for a subsequent housebreaking and was sentenced on both complaints on the same day to six months' imprisonment on each complaint, the sentences to be consecutive, the submission that the sentences should have been concurrent was dismissed by the appeal court as being of no weight; the sentences were deemed to have been entirely proper.[69] No guidance was given on whether it would have made any difference had the charge on the second complaint been committed before those on the first, in which case the Crown would have been able to incorporate it in the first complaint.

Where an offender appeared on three complaints on the same day and was sentenced to six months' imprisonment on each, the sentences to run consecutively, the appeal court upheld the disposal. The offender had appeared in a sheriff summary court in September 1986 and in November 1986 a summary warrant was granted for an offence committed that month. A further offence committed on 29 December led to his appearance in court on all three complaints on 30 December 1986. The appeal court considered that the sheriff had addressed his mind to the question of why the offender had appeared on separate complaints and was satisfied that equity did not require the three complaints to be treated as one.[70]

4.13.3 Bail. It is quite proper to make a sentence in respect of breach of bail conditions consecutive to sentences imposed for other offences. To order the sentences to run concurrently would result in the offender receiving no punishment for contravening the Bail Act, so that it might be wrong for a judge to do other than to order the sentences to run consecutively.[71] Sentences imposed for contravention of the Bail Act should therefore normally be made consecutive to any sentences imposed in respect of other charges on the same complaint or indictment. It would be for the accused to show cause why the sentences should not be ordered to run consecutively. In particular, a sentence imposed in respect of a contravention of

s. 3(1) (*a*) of the Bail Act ought to be ordered to run consecutively or the result would be that the accused would suffer no penalty for failing to appear at a diet of which he had been given due notice.[72]

If an accused person has been granted bail on more than one occasion and subsequently commits an offence, the Crown may libel the breaches of the different bail orders as separate charges. As it would be the same offence which constituted the breach of the order in each case, any custodial sentences imposed on the bail charges may be made concurrent to each other.[73] However, when an accused faces breaches of two or more bail orders on one complaint, it is competent for the judge to order the sentences in respect of the bail contraventions to run consecutively. Whether the sentences imposed should run consecutively or concurrently is a matter for the judge's discretion.[74] It has been suggested that it would be for the accused to show that the judge had erred in his discretion in making the sentences consecutive, not for the judge to explain why he did not make them concurrent.[75]

4.13.4   Life imprisonment. It is not appropriate to impose a sentence of imprisonment consecutive to a life sentence since a life sentence is never extinguished or spent.[76] Sentences on those already sentenced to and serving life imprisonment should therefore be made to run from the date on which the sentence is imposed.[77]

4.13.5   Similar offences. It may be appropriate for sentences of imprisonment in respect of very similar offences to be made concurrent. The appeal court has altered consecutive sentences imposed on an offender for two thefts committed by opening a lockfast meter and has made them concurrent.[78]

4.13.6   Same incident. Where the charges arise out of the same incident, it may be more appropriate to make the sentences imposed concurrent.[79]

4.13.7   Contempt of court. A sentence of contempt of court can be made consecutive to a sentence currently being served for a crime.[80] It is within the court's inherent power, otherwise contempt of court by a witness serving a long prison sentence might virtually go unpunished. It may exceed the limit which the court would otherwise be able to impose.[81]

4.13.8 Common law powers. Under s. 430(4) of the 1975 Act a consecutive sentence can be made to take effect only at the expiry of any previous sentence which at the date of conviction the offender was undergoing. Where an offender pled guilty and sentence had been deferred, it was once considered to have been incompetent to order a sentence of imprisonment to run consecutively to a sentence which had earlier been imposed but which was subsequent to the plea being tendered.[82] However, the Court of Criminal Appeal has since made clear that the date of conviction for these purposes is not the date of the plea of guilty but the date of the sentence.[83] Section 430(4), therefore, does not operate as a restriction on the courts' common law powers to impose consecutive sentences. There is no difference between consecutive sentences imposed on the same day and sentences ordered to run from the expiry of a sentence previously imposed.[84]

4.13.9 Consecutive sentences of detention as child and in young offenders institution. For the purposes of releasing a person on licence, consecutive terms of imprisonment or detention to which a person has been sentenced are treated as a single term – except in the case of release on licence where the sentence was one of detention of a child convicted on indictment.[85] The result is that a person who was sentenced as a child after conviction on indictment to be detained for a period exceeding 18 months would be eligible to be released on licence.[86] However, if he was sentenced to a period of detention in a young offenders institution to run consecutively to the period of detention as a child, he would have to serve all of the sentence of detention as a child and two-thirds of the sentence of detention at the young offenders institution before he could be released.

The question of whether the legislation should be amended has been aired by the Court of Criminal Appeal, but meantime it recommends that judges should bear in mind that it would be more appropriate for some other method of disposal to be adopted rather than imposing a consecutive sentence. If this was done, then account could be taken of the disposal when consideration was being given to releasing the person on licence.[87]

4.13.10 Accused already serving two or more sentences. Where an accused person is already serving two or more consecutive sentences and is about to be given an additional sentence which is to be made consecutive to the total of the sentences previously imposed, the judge should provide that the sentence being imposed is to be "consecutive to the total period of imprisonment to which the prisoner is already subject" or "is to take effect on the expiry of all sentences previously imposed".[88]

4.13.11 Abandoned appeal. When an appeal against a custodial sentence in a summary case is abandoned by an appellant who is on bail, the lower court has power to imprison him for the unexpired period of his sentence.[89] In such a case, where the person is already serving a term of imprisonment imposed subsequent to the conviction appealed against, the court may order the sentence to run from such date as the court may think fit, not later than the date on which the term of imprisonment subsequently imposed expires.[90]

When a judge is contemplating ordering that the unexpired portion of the sentence appealed against should run other than concurrently, intimation should be given to the offender, who should make any representations he wishes in writing, personally or through a solicitor. On receipt of such representations the judge may decide whether or not to hold a hearing.[91] If the sentence is to be made consecutive the accused would require to be present, since all sentences must be imposed in the presence of the accused.[92]

4.14 Non-legally represented offender

A court is restricted in imposing a custodial sentence in respect of an offence or imposing the alternative of imprisonment or detention in respect of failure to pay a fine if the accused is not legally represented and has not previously received a custodial sentence in the United Kingdom. In these circumstances it may only do so if the accused has already been refused legal aid on the ground that he was not financially eligible or has been informed of his right to apply for legal aid but has refused to do so.[93] If a non-legally represented offender was not informed of his right to apply for legal aid, a custodial sentence imposed on him could not stand.[94]

4.15   Backdating

In passing a sentence of imprisonment or detention, a court must in determining the period of imprisonment or detention have regard to any period of time spent in custody by the offender on remand awaiting trial or sentence.[95]

There is no rule that a judge is required to backdate a sentence, provided that he has regard to the period of time spent in custody on remand. He may backdate or he may have regard to the time spent in custody on remand when selecting the appropriate period of a sentence and adjust the sentence accordingly.[96] This would be so even if an offender remained in custody on remand for almost 110 days and then pled guilty on the morning of the trial.[97]

In an earlier decision the Court of Criminal Appeal had held that it was entirely a matter within the judge's discretion whether or not a sentence should be backdated.[98] This has since been modified to the effect that the discretion would have to be exercised properly. It is not sufficient to say that the offender's time in custody prior to his trial was entirely of his own making because he refused to admit his guilt. A person is entitled to plead not guilty and to insist on going to trial. The fact that he does not do so is not a reason for a judge refusing to backdate his sentence upon his conviction.[99]

There is no rule that in every case where there has been a continuation for background reports any sentence imposed must be backdated.[100] In general, if an offender is remanded in custody for reports and the sentence then imposed is the maximum available, it might be appropriate to backdate the sentence in order that the period on remand be taken into account.[101] However, if the remand in custody to enable reports to be prepared is brought about by the person's persistent offending, a judge would be entitled to exercise his discretion not to backdate.[102]

If a person is detained in custody due to the seriousness of the charges and is ultimately convicted only of reduced charges on which in all probability he would have been allowed bail had those been the offences originally charged, it would be appropriate for any sentence to be backdated.[103]

Where an offender was prepared to plead guilty from the time when he was apprehended but did not in fact do so until the morning of the trial, the appeal court held that the sentence should have been backdated.[104]

In the case of a s. 102 letter being tendered, where the judge is to backdate the sentence, he should generally do so from the date when the s. 102 letter was signed.[105]

In a case where an offender at his first appearance offered to plead guilty to a reduced charge and that plea was not accepted by the Crown but where subsequently the Crown did accept a plea in substantially similar terms, it was held that the sentence should have been backdated to the date of his first appearance.[106]

4.16　Revocation of licence by court

If a person released from prison on parole is convicted of an offence punishable on indictment with imprisonment, the court may, whether or not it imposes any other sentence, revoke the parole licence.[107]

Notes

1. 1975 Act, s. 221.
2. 1975 Act, ss. 207(1) and 415(1). (Ss. 207 and 415 were substituted by the 1980 Act, s. 45, Sch. 6 para. 5 and further amended by the 1980 Act, s. 124 and S.I. 1983 No. 1580, art. 3.) See 1975 Act, ss. 212 and 421 on recall to young offenders institutions of those released under supervision from detention to reconviction. See also para. 4.13.9.
3. 1975 Act, ss. 207(2) and 415(2).
4. 1975 Act, ss. 207(5) and 415(5).
5. *Dunsmore* v. *Allan* 1991 S.C.C.R. 946.
6. *Ibid.*
7. 1975 Act, ss. 207(3) and (4) and 415(3) and (4).
8. *Milligan* v. *Jessop* 1988 S.C.C.R. 137.
9. 1975 Act, ss. 173 (as amended by the 1980 Act, Sch. 7 para. 35) and 372. See para. 5.10.
10. 1975 Act, s. 206(1). S. 206 was substituted by the 1980 Act, s. 44.
11. 1975 Act, s. 206(2). See also 1975 Act, s. 206A as inserted by the Law Reform (Miscellaneous Provisions) Act 1985, s. 45.
12. *K.* v. *H.M. Advocate* 1991 S.C.C.R. 703.
13. 1975 Act, s. 206(3); Prisons (Scotland) Act 1989, s. 25.
14. *Clayton, Petitioner* 1991 S.C.C.R. 261; 1992 S.L.T. 404. See para. 4.13.9.
15. 1975 Act, s. 413(1) and (2) as substituted by the Criminal Justice (Scotland) Act 1987, s. 59(1).
16. 1975 Act, ss. 2(2) and 221(1) as amended by the Criminal Justice (Scotland) Act 1987, s. 58.
17. *Moore* v. *H.M. Advocate* 1989 S.C.C.R. 298; 1989 S.L.T. 883.

18. 1975 Act, s. 289(d). Further provisions relating to maximum periods fixed in particular statutes are set out in ss. 289B (as added by the Criminal Law Act 1977, s. 63(1) and substituted by the Criminal Justice Act 1982, s. 55(2)) and 289E (as added by the Criminal Justice Act 1982, s. 54).

19. *Fairbairn* v. *Drummond* (1836) 1 Swinton 85; *Fraser* v. *Herron* 1968 J.C. 1; 1968 S.L.T. 149. See para. 6.1.6.

20. 1975 Act, s. 290; *Hemphill* v. *Donnelly* 1992 S.C.C.R. 770.

21. *Adair* v. *Morton* 1972 S.L.T. (Notes) 70.

22. *Sharp* v. *Tudhope* 1986 S.C.C.R. 64.

23. 1975 Act, s. 104(1) as inserted by the 1980 Act, s. 12, Sch. 4 para. 15 and amended by the Criminal Justice (Scotland) Act 1987, s. 58(2).

24. 1975 Act, s. 104(1A).

25. *H.M. Advocate* v. *Stern* 1974 S.L.T. 2; *H.M. Advocate* v. *Anderson* 1946 J.C. 81.

26. *H.M. Advocate* v. *Duffy* 1954 S.L.T. (Notes) 46.

27. 1975 Act, s. 284(a).

28. 1980 Act, s. 79(1) as amended by the Criminal Justice Act 1982, s. 56(3), Schs. 7 and 16.

29. 1975 Act, s. 284(d).

30. *Duffy* v. *Lakie* 1962 S.L.T. 30.

31. *Beattie* v. *H.M. Advocate* 1986 S.C.C.R. 605. *cf. Beattie, Ptnr* 1992 S.C.C.R. 812.

32. 1980 Act, s. 42(1).

33. 1980 Act, s. 42(2).

34. See further paras. 4.2 and 4.3.

35. *Hamilton* v. *Hillary* 1986 S.C.C.R. 114.

36. *Flood* v. *McLeod* 1983 S.C.C.R. 387.

37. *Cluness* v. *Allan* 1984 S.C.C.R. 205.

38. *Pearson* v. *H.M. Advocate* 1990 S.C.C.R. 125.

39. *Havlin* v. *H.M. Advocate* 1990 S.C.C.R. 467.

40. *Gordon* v. *Hamilton* 1987 S.C.C.R. 146.

41. *Gibson* v. *Annan* 1990 S.C.C.R. 519.

42. *Crilley* v. *MacDougall* 1986 S.C.C.R. 587. See also *MacRae* v. *H.M. Advocate* 1987 S.C.C.R. 712.

43. *Selfridge* v. *H.M. Advocate* 1981 S.C.C.R. 223.

44. *Smith* v. *Wilson* 1987 S.C.C.R. 191.

45. *Bennett* v. *Tudhope* 1987 S.C.C.R. 203.

46. *Donnelly* v. *Hamilton* 1987 S.C.C.R. 313.

47. *Murchie* v. *McGlennan* 1990 S.C.C.R. 533.

48. *Donaldson* v. *H.M. Advocate* 1983 S.C.C.R. 216. For the implications of a life sentence on consecutive sentences see para. 4.13.4.

49. *Allan* v. *H.M. Advocate* 1983 S.C.C.R. 183.

50. *Donaldson* v. *H.M. Advocate* 1983 S.C.C.R. 216.

51. *Duff* v. *H.M. Advocate* 1983 S.C.C.R. 461. See also *K.* v. *H.M. Advocate* 1991 S.C.C.R. 703.

52. *Townsley* v. *H.M. Advocate* 1986 S.C.C.R. 248.

53. *Robertson* v. *H.M. Advocate* 1987 S.C.C.R. 385.

54. 1975 Act, s. 425(1).

55. *McKenzie* v. *Lockhart* 1986 S.C.C.R. 663.

56. *Kinney* v. *Tudhope* 1985 S.C.C.R. 393.

57. *Stirling* v. *Stewart* 1988 S.C.C.R. 619.

58. 1975 Act, s. 424 as amended by the 1980 Act, s. 84(2), Sch. 7 para. 68 and S.I. 1983 No. 1580, art. 3.

59. 1975 Act, s. 430(4), relating to summary proceedings; *Grey* v. *H.M. Advocate* 1958 S.L.T. 147.

60. *Wishart* v. *Heatly* 1953 J.C. 42; 1953 S.L.T. 184; *Maguiness* v. *MacDonald* 1953 J.C. 31; 1953 S.L.T. 158.
61. *H.M. Advocate* v. *Logan* (1972) S.C.C.R. Supp. 26.
62. 1975 S.L.T. (Notes) 92.
63. *McGory* v. *Jessop* 1990 S.C.C.R. 222. See *Ross* v. *McLeod* 1987 S.C.C.R. 525.
64. *Moore* v. *H.M. Advocate* 1989 S.C.C.R. 298; 1989 S.L.T. 883.
65. *Hunt* v. *Wilson* 1991 S.C.C.R. 821.
66. *Thomson* v. *Smith* 1982 J.C. 40; 1982 S.C.C.R. 57; 1982 S.L.T. 546.
67. *Ibid.*
68. *Ibid.*
69. *Haggerty* v. *Tudhope* 1985 S.C.C.R. 121.
70. *O'Lone* v. *Tudhope* 1987 S.C.C.R. 211.
71. *Allan* v. *Lockhart* 1986 S.C.C.R. 395; *Garner* v. *Lockhart* 1990 S.C.C.R. 385.
72. *Kelso* v. *Crowe* 1992 S.C.C.R. 415.
73. *Allan* v. *Lockhart* 1986 S.C.C.R. 395; *Montgomery* v. *H.M. Advocate* 1987 S.C.C.R. 264.
74. *Whyte* v. *Normand* 1988 S.C.C.R. 465.
75. *Ibid.*, the Commentary thereon.
76. *McRae* v. *H.M. Advocate* 1987 S.C.C.R. 36.
77. *McPhee* v. *H.M. Advocate* 1990 S.C.C.R. 313.
78. *Allan* v. *Lockhart* 1986 S.C.C.R. 395. See also *Brodie* v. *H.M. Advocate* 1992 S.C.C.R. 487.
79. *McGuigan* v. *Wilson* 1988 S.C.C.R. 474; *Sillars* v. *H.M. Advocate* 1990 S.C.C.R. 425.
80. *Manson, Petitioner* (1977) S.C.C.R. Supp. 176.
81. *Young* v. *McGlennan* 1990 S.C.C.R. 373; 1991 S.L.T. 375.
82. *Noble* v. *Guild* 1987 S.C.C.R. 518.
83. *Beattie* v. *McGlennan* 1990 S.C.C.R. 497; 1991 S.L.T. 384.
84. *Russell* v. *MacPhail* 1990 J.C. 380; 1990 S.C.C.R. 628; 1991 S.L.T. 449.
85. Prisons (Scotland) Act 1989, s. 43(2).
86. 1975 Act, s. 206(2) and (3) as substituted by the 1980 Act, s. 44.
87. *Clayton, Petitioner* 1991 S.C.C.R. 261; 1992 S.L.T. 404.
88. *Moore* v. *McPhail* 1986 S.C.C.R. 669.
89. 1975 Act, s. 446(4) as amended by the Bail etc. (Scotland) Act 1980, Sch. 1 para. 11.
90. 1975 Act, s. 446(5) as amended by the Bail etc. (Scotland) Act 1980, Sch. 1 para. 11.
91. *Proudfoot* v. *Wither* 1990 J.C. 238; 1990 S.C.C.R. 96; 1990 S.L.T. 742.
92. 1975 Act, s. 433.
93. Criminal Justice (Scotland) Act 1980, s. 41(1).
94. *Milligan* v. *Jessop* 1988 S.C.C.R. 137.
95. 1975 Act, ss. 218 and 431 as amended by the 1980 Act, s. 83(2) and (3), Sch. 7 paras. 40 and 7, Sch. 8.
96. *Neilson* v. *H.M. Advocate* 1989 S.C.C.R. 527. See also *Bellamy* v. *H.M. Advocate* 1987 S.C.C.R. 101; *Cannon* v. *H.M. Advocate* 1991 S.L.T. 195.
97. *Dallas* v. *H.M. Advocate* 1992 S.C.C.R. 40.
98. *Muir* v. *H.M. Advocate* 1985 S.C.C.R. 402.
99. *Grummer* v. *H.M. Advocate* 1991 S.C.C.R. 194; *Wojciechowski* v. *McLeod* 1992 S.C.C.R. 563. See generally "Backdating" and "Backdating – New Developments", 1991 S.L.T. 23 and 93.
100. *McDonald* v. *Wilson* 1991 S.C.C.R. 61; *Morrison* v. *Scott* 1987 S.C.C.R. 376 commented upon.
101. *Morrison* v. *Scott* 1987 S.C.C.R. 376.

102. *Brady* v. *McNeill* 1991 S.C.C.R. 234; *McDonald* v. *Wilson* 1991 S.C.C.R. 61.
103. *Callaghan* v. *H.M. Advocate* 1986 S.C.C.R. 563.
104. *Campbell* v. *H.M. Advocate* 1986 S.C.C.R. 403.
105. *Neilson* v. *H.M. Advocate* 1989 S.C.C.R. 527.
106. *Tulloch* v. *Annan* 1991 S.C.C.R. 24.
107. 1975 Act, ss. 213 and 422. See also 1975 Act, ss. 214 and 423 on failure to comply with conditions of supervision.

CHAPTER 5

NON-CUSTODIAL MEASURES

5.1 Absolute discharge

5.1.1 General. Where a person is convicted in solemn proceedings of an offence (other than an offence the sentence for which is fixed by law), the court may, instead of sentencing him, make an order discharging him absolutely. It may do so where it is of the opinion, having regard to the circumstances, including the nature of the offence and the character of the offender, that it was inexpedient to inflict punishment and that a probation order was not appropriate.[1]

A summary court has a similar power which is exercised where the court is satisfied that the person committed the offence but without proceeding to conviction.[2] As a summary court when granting an absolute discharge does not proceed to conviction, there is no conviction to appeal against. Formerly, it was not possible to appeal against the court's finding by way of a note of appeal.[3] However, s. 392(4) of the 1975 Act now gives the same right of appeal against a finding leading to an absolute discharge as against conviction.

As a forfeiture order proceeds upon a conviction,[4] forfeiture is not an appropriate disposal along with an absolute discharge in a summary case.

5.1.2 Effects of order. If a person is discharged absolutely the conviction is deemed not to be a conviction for any purpose other than the purposes of the proceedings in which the order was made and of laying it before a court as a previous conviction in a subsequent case.[5] It may therefore be a more appropriate disposal than an admonition.[6]

Any absolute discharge is disregarded for the purposes of any enactment which imposes any disqualification or disability upon convicted persons or authorises or requires the imposition of such disqualification or disability.[7] However, it is now

competent to combine absolute discharge with disqualification.[8]
It is also competent when granting an absolute discharge to
exclude an accused from licensed premises,[9] to recommend that
he be deported[10] or that tools and implements for use in theft
are to be forfeited.[11]

Where a person has previously been discharged absolutely, it
is competent in subsequent proceedings to bring the absolute
discharge order before the court in like manner as if the order
were a conviction.[12]

5.2 Admonition

If it appears to meet the justice of the case, a court may dismiss
with an admonition any person found guilty of an offence.[13]

5.3 Community service

5.3.1 General. It was in the report of the Wootton Committee that the introduction of community service was first
recommended in the United Kingdom, subsequently being
made available for England and Wales in the Criminal Justice
Act 1972.[14] In Scotland, after schemes had been set up on an
experimental basis in four areas whereby the imposition of a
number of hours of unpaid work for the community could be
added as a condition to a probation order, community service
was made available by the Community Service by Offenders
(Scotland) Act 1978.[15] Community service is now available as a
sentencing option throughout Scotland for the High Court of
Justiciary and sheriff courts.

On 1 April 1989 the Social Work Services Group of the Scottish
Office published new national standards for the operation of
community service schemes in Scotland. One of the main aims
of the national standards was to promote further the use of
community service as an alternative for offenders who would
otherwise have been sentenced to imprisonment. There has also
been a study carried out following upon the publication of the
national standards on the perception of community service by
sentencers.[16] The achievement of the aim of applying a
community service order in place of a sentence of imprisonment
is ultimately in the hands of the sentencers and so this study has
sought to assess the perceptions of Scottish sentencers towards
community service as a disposal. There has been a changeover

to full central funding of community service schemes and an increase in the number of places available is scheduled.

5.3.2 Purposes. The purpose of community service is sometimes seen as keeping the offender out of prison. However, that is not enshrined in the legislation establishing community service schemes. Section 1 of the 1978 Act made community service available where an offender aged 16 years or over was convicted of an offence punishable by imprisonment, other than murder. It enabled the courts to impose a community service order instead of dealing with the offender in any other way. The Act, therefore, does not state that community service is to be imposed as an alternative to custody. It limits the offences in respect of which community service may be imposed. As community service involves a considerable outlay of resources in assessing candidates and supervising work, it is not considered to be an appropriate option for trivial offences.

The CRU Paper reported that 80 per cent of the sheriffs in the sample considered that community service should be used primarily where the offence and circumstances would otherwise have warranted a custodial sentence.[17] The remaining 20 per cent preferred to adopt a more flexible approach, even if this involved using the disposal instead of fines or other non-custodial options.

The Wootton Committee viewed community service as having several objectives, namely to punish the offender, to reform him and to make constructive use of resources. Community service would punish the offender by encroaching upon his free time and making him apply that time in a socially useful way. It could therefore be retributive in making the punishment fit the crime, although this would not now be attempted. The punishment would be constructive, involving work which was potentially of benefit to the community at large and also might have some rehabilitative effect on the individual by bringing him into contact with others in need of help. Moreoever, it was a constructive use of resources if used as an alternative to imprisonment, thereby relieving the pressures on overcrowded prisons.

Such were the lofty aims of the community service scheme.

Their multiplicity and vagueness may have made it more difficult
to establish any clear, single purpose for a community service
order. However, its ability to satisfy a number of objectives can be
perceived as one of its attractions, providing a punitive response
while at the same time having some positive aspects.

The variety of roles of community service can be problematic.
In *McCusker* v. *H.M. Advocate* the sheriff pointed out that
community service was designed to assist the rehabilitation of an
offender and he had difficulty in seeing how that could be
achieved in the case of an offender who maintained his innocence
and displayed no remorse or contrition.[18] The appeal court
observed that it was not a prerequisite to the making of a
community service order that an accused person should have
displayed remorse or contrition.

5.3.3 Procedure. A community service order may be
accompanied by disqualification from driving, caution, forfeiture
or a compensation order but not with any other sentence.[19]
Before making an order the court must obtain a report from the
local authority and be satisfied that the offender is suitable for the
work and that there is work for him to do.[20] The court should
explain the purpose and effect of the order to the offender and
obtain his consent to it.[21] An order can be made concurrently with
or consecutive to another community service order but the total
number of hours may not exceed 240.[22] Arrangements have been
made for the reciprocal enforcement of community service orders
within the United Kingdom.[23]

5.3.4 Community service and imprisonment. Although s. 1(1)
of the 1978 Act provides that the court may make a community
service order where a person is convicted of an offence
punishable by imprisonment "instead of dealing with him in
any other way", where a person appears on more than one
complaint this does not apply to all matters then before the
court. In *McQueen* v. *Lockhart* the appellant had appeared before
the sheriff court on two complaints.[24] He was ordered to
perform 120 hours' community service on one and sentenced to
60 days' detention on the second. The court held that there was
no basis for treating the two complaints as one and so the
sentences were competent.

The seriousness of the offence may call for a more severe

penalty than community service. In *McCusker* v. *H.M. Advocate* the sheriff imposed a sentence of four months' imprisonment for theft by housebreaking along with others of 119,000 cigarettes, mainly because of the seriousness of the offence which he described as carefully planned and professionally executed. The appeal court held that he was entitled to reject community service and impose a custodial sentence in view of the gravity of the offence.

Where a very serious offence had been committed for which a custodial sentence was appropriate, the appeal court has stated that it could only quash that sentence if satisfied that the accused would benefit from a period of community service as a direct alternative to custody.[25]

5.3.5 Community service and probation. As a legacy from the experimental schemes, by the time that community service came to be introduced in Scotland in 1978 a linkage was maintained between community service and probation orders. Section 7 of the 1978 Act amended ss. 183 and 384 of the 1975 Act, enabling a court in making a probation order to require that the offender perform community service.

This option does not appear to be widely used in practice, despite one sheriff participating in the CRU Paper describing it as his "ideal sentence". Its appeal was seen to lie in its ability to combine the "punitive" element of sentencing with the "therapeutic" support and guidance provided by a social worker. It may be used where the offender requires additional supervision and assistance or instead of a probation order alone where the seriousness of the offence merits a further sanction. However, it is not available as yet throughout the country but only in approximately half of the court districts.

5.3.6 Employment. Whether a person about to be sentenced is in employment can in practice be of relevance to the sentence imposed, although it may be questionable whether it should be. Those in employment in general are less likely to receive a custodial sentence.

In a similar vein, the CRU Paper found that an offender's employment status could have an influence upon the imposition of a community service order. This was partly because someone who was unemployed would be more free to carry out community service and could perform a higher number of hours and partly because it was thought by some sentencers that performing unpaid work in the community could give some offenders "a new sense of purpose, self-respect and self-discipline".[26] The alternative view was that employment should have no bearing in deciding upon community service, the number of hours being commensurate with the gravity of the offence and the offender's previous convictions.

5.3.7 Changes to community service orders. A community service order may be altered or revoked on the application of the offender or the local authority officer if it appears in the interests of justice to do so.[27] Normally, the work must be completed within 12 months[28] but the court has power to extend this. It may also vary the number of hours or revoke the order and impose some other sentence if the offender had made an application to this effect or, where the application is made by the officer, the offender has been cited to appear before the court.[29] Arrangements may also be made to perform the community service in another locality.[30]

5.3.8 Expiry of community service orders. There has been some confusion as to the termination of community service orders. The clearest way of bringing them to a conclusion would be where the community service was successfully performed. The confusion has arisen as a result of the wording of s. 3(2) of the 1978 Act which provides that the work is to be performed during the period of 12 months from the date of the order and that unless revoked the order shall remain in force until completed. Lord Justice-General Emslie in *H.M. Advocate* v. *Hood* commented that the language of the section "can only be described as clumsy".[31]

The conclusion which the court reached in that case, which was the best that the court believed that the language of s. 3(2) would permit and was best calculated to achieve all of the purposes of the Act, was to decide that the 12 month period was the time in which the offender might lawfully be required to perform work under the order but that the second part kept the order in force. This meant that it was open to the community service officer to apply to the court under s. 5 to have the 12 month period extended, even after the expiry of that period.

Thereafter the court could find the individual in breach of the order, revoke it and deal with him *de novo*.

This has clarified the way in which the provisions are to be interpreted but still means that matters are unlikely to be straightforward in practice. In *H.M. Advocate* v. *Hood* it meant that the complaint was irrelevant since the 12 month period had not been extended and so the appellant could not have been required to carry out work under the order.

5.3.9 Breach of community service. If the offender fails to comply with the order the local authority officer may report that to the court and the court may grant a warrant to arrest or cite the offender.[32] On his appearance in court the offender will be asked whether he admits or denies the breach. If he admits it or if it is proved that he has failed without reasonable excuse to comply with any requirement of the order the court may impose a fine and continue the order, revoke the order and sentence him again or vary the number of hours.[33] It has been held in the sheriff court that it is not competent to sentence an offender in breach of a community service order in the absence of the principal complaint.[34]

Those participating in the CRU Paper indicated that in the event of an offender returning to court in breach of a community service order a custodial sentence would probably ensue unless plausible reasons were presented in mitigation. Four main criteria were seen as being influential: the nature of the offence, the reasons for the breach, the proportion of the order completed and the motivation and commitment of the offender.

This is in line with a recent appeal against a custodial sentence for breach of community service where the Court of Criminal Appeal proposed that a firm view should be taken in the event of a breach, indicating that in cases of default the sanction of custody will generally be applied. In *Dunsmure* v. *Lowe* the appellant was sentenced to 60 hours' community service.[35] Thereafter he served a prison sentence, was in hospital and changed his address more than once and did not perform any of his community service. When reported for breach of it he was sentenced to 60 days' imprisonment, with which the appeal court would not interfere. For non-custodial sentencing options to be successful, it was considered necessary that they be backed up by the imposition of a sentence of imprisonment if not taken advantage of.

However, this is not an absolute rule. In *Rankin* v. *McGlennan* the appellant had completed 12½ hours' service out of 240 hours.[36] After being reported for breach of it she was sentenced to three months' detention. The appeal court did quash the sentence of detention and imposed a £300 fine since she was then in a position to pay a substantial fine.

Again, in *Simpson* v. *H.M. Advocate* the appellant was sentenced to six months' imprisonment after being in breach of an order to perform 200 hours of community service.[37] Although the sheriff was considered to have been entitled to regard the appellant's disregard of the opportunities to complete the order as flagrant, the court was prepared with great reluctance to quash the prison sentence and substitute an order for 240 hours of community service. In the interim he had obtained new employment which made it easier to perform community service.

The appeal court may therefore be seen to have indicated its general view on the implications of breach of community service but to be willing to entertain exceptions to that approach.

5.3.10   Tariff escalation. Community service is seen by many as an offender's last chance. If he does not mend his ways he may in future expect a custodial sentence. This is especially the view of those who see community service as an alternative to imprisonment. Accordingly, many courts will not impose community service on more than one occasion on the same offender.[38]

This gives rise to a problem if community service is used in some courts as an alternative to non-custodial sentences. If used in this way, the offender may be placed at greater risk of custody if he returns to court for breaching the order or if he makes a subsequent appearance in court on another charge. If not careful, the imposition of a community service order could have the effect of moving some offenders prematurely up the sentencing scale. The only way of preventing this would be if the subsequent sentencer knew why the earlier order had been imposed. However, this would not be apparent and would require some further knowledge of the earlier case.

5.3.11   The number of hours. The minimum number of hours of community service which may be ordered is 40 and the maximum number is 240.[39] The number may be amended by order of the Secretary of State.[40] While the opinion of those participating in the CRU Paper study was divided, most were of the view that increasing the number of hours would make no significant difference.[41] There was a perception that if an order for 240 hours did no good, one for more would fare no better. Community service was not seen as a suitable alternative to custody for serious cases on indictment.

Although the maximum number of hours is 240, this should not be used indiscriminately but only in the more severe of cases for which community service would be appropriate. In *Brown* v. *Normand* the appellant had been sentenced to 240 hours of community service.[42] Both he and the complainer had been at a party when a fight broke out and he had been asked to leave. He was chased by a crowd which included the complainer. When the crowd turned to go back to the house the appellant threw a brick at them which injured the complainer. In the circumstances, it was held that the number of hours in the community service order was excessive and it was reduced to 100.

5.3.12 District courts. The district court clerks and justices participating in the CRU Paper were keen to see community service available at district court level. In two of the locations community service was available while in the other three those involved would have liked to have acquired the facility.[43] However, since custodial sentences are rare in the district court, community service would be used as an alternative to a fine. It may be attractive to justices to be able to impose a short period of community service; 20 hours may suffice, although the present minimum would have to be reduced. However, it has been found that the expenses of short community service orders are proportionately far higher than longer ones and that community service is more costly than a short prison sentence.[44] Against this must be borne the capability of the district court to impose a prison sentence of up to 60 days.[45] In particular, the stipendiary magistrate may see the benefit of being able to impose a community service order in place of a custodial sentence.

5.3.13 The use of community service orders. Several conflicts are apparent in relation to a community service order, perhaps due to the multiplicity of its roles. It would appear that the Social Work Services Group see its value as being an alternative to imprisonment. By keeping a greater number of offenders out of prison, community service orders have a diversionary impact. High Court judges and sheriffs, while using community service as an alternative to imprisonment, desire to be able to use it as part of their range of options. For their part, district court justices would like to see their sentencing options increased even if this would involve a change in the way in which community service orders were utilised.

Since their introduction, the number of community service orders imposed has increased slightly from, for example, 2,430 cases in 1984 to 3,351 in 1988, an increase from 1.3 per cent to 1.9 per cent of all disposals.[46] With more places being made available the number may be expected to rise further.

5.4 Death sentence

A capital sentence is no longer competent for murder and is not competent under the 1975 Act.[47] Although the death sentence would now only be competent in respect of treason, were that ever to be charged, there is still a prescribed form of death sentence and relative procedure.[48]

5.5 Deferred sentence

5.5.1 General. A court may defer sentence after conviction for a period on such conditions as it may determine. The fact that the accused has been convicted does not prevent the court from making a probation order in due course.

If a person on whom sentence has been deferred is convicted during the period of deferment by a court in any part of Great Britain of an offence committed during that period and has been dealt with for that offence, the original court may issue a warrant for his arrest or cite him to appear before it. The court may then deal with him in any manner in which it would have been competent for it to have dealt with him on the expiry of the period of deferment.

A court which has deferred sentence on a person and which convicts that person of another offence during the period of deferment may deal with him for the original offence in any manner in which it would have been competent for it to have dealt with him on the expiry of the period of deferment, as well as for the offence committed during that period.[49]

A court should not defer sentence on an offender for the purpose of obtaining social enquiry and community service reports as a means of circumventing the three week period of adjourning the diet for reports laid down in s. 179(1) of the 1975 Act.[50] Nor should a judge use his power to defer sentence in order to get round what he perceives as the incompetence of imposing consecutive periods of imprisonment.[51]

A custodial sentence should not be imposed on one charge on a complaint or indictment with sentence deferred on another.[52]

5.5.2 Custody after deferment. Where a judge defers sentence and indicates to the offender that if he is of good behaviour he will not receive a custodial sentence, a prison sentence ought not to be imposed at the end of the deferment if he has been of good behaviour.[53] However, a judge should not tie his hands by promising to impose a specific sentence if the accused commits any offence in the interim period. The judge ought to consider the situation anew at the end of the period of deferment.[54]

A sentence of one year's detention after deferment of sentence for six months for good behaviour was not considered by the appeal court to be excessive. The offender had not committed any further crimes in the interim but had not co-operated in the preparation of the social enquiry report and had continued to be amused by the offence and to express no concern for the victims, as had been his attitude at the original hearing. He had demonstrated a total lack of concern for other people and a total lack of understanding of the gravity of the crime (assault and robbery) which he had planned and committed.[55]

5.5.3 Conditions of deferment obtempered. Where sentence has been deferred for good behaviour, the court may ultimately merely impose an admonition. However, the court still has a discretion as to the appropriate sentence to impose and may in certain circumstances justifiably impose, for example, a fine.[56] Where the original offence was a breach of the peace and the accused was of good behaviour for a year, the Court of Criminal Appeal considered a fine of £100 to be excessive; it was quashed and an admonition substituted.[57]

5.5.4 Same judge. If a judge places an offender on deferred sentence, when the offender reappears on the expiry of the period of deferment, he should be dealt with by the same judge unless the exigencies of business demand that that should not be the case.[58]

5.6 Deportation

A person who is not a British citizen is liable to deportation from the United Kingdom if, after he has attained the age of 17, he is convicted of an offence for which he is punishable with imprisonment and on his conviction is recommended for deportation.[59]

Deportation should be recommended only in relation to a serious charge or a succession of charges indicating a course of conduct. The test is whether allowing the offender to remain in the country would be contrary to the national interest. In the case of a Community national the test is expressed as being whether the offender's continued presence in the United Kingdom would be a genuine and sufficiently serious threat affecting one of the fundamental interests of society. A simple assault by a person with minor previous convictions would not merit a recommendation for deportation, there being no possible danger to the safety of the country.[60]

A fraud on a bank may be sufficiently serious to merit deportation. Where a Nigerian came to Scotland to study but while here opened false bank accounts and then drew a number of cheques in quick succession exceeding the amount of money deposited, the court considered that the offences seriously undermined the system of running current accounts in banks and that a recommendation for deportation was justified.[61]

A recommendation for deportation was also held to be justified in respect of 16 convictions for fraud in addition to three previous convictions for dishonesty. There was considered to be a continuing course of conduct extending over several months, which was likely to be repeated in the future to the detriment of the community.[62]

Conversely, a minor theft and giving a false name to the police are not sufficiently serious to merit deportation.[63]

5.7 Guardianship

Where a person is convicted in the High Court of Justiciary or the sheriff court of an offence which is punishable by imprisonment, other than an offence the sentence for which is fixed by law, the court may place him under the guardianship of a local authority or a person approved by a local authority specified in the order.[64]

5.8 Hospital order

Equally, where a person is convicted in the High Court of Justiciary or the sheriff court of an offence which is punishable by imprisonment, other than an offence the sentence for which is fixed by law, the court may make a hospital order authorising his admission to and detention in a hospital specified in the order.[65] The High Court and sheriff court also have power to make interim hospital orders.[66]

Before making a hospital order, the court must be satisfied that grounds set out in s. 17(1) or s. 36(a) of the Mental Health (Scotland) Act 1984 apply in relation to the offender and be of the opinion that the most suitable method of disposing of the case is by means of a hospital order.[67] An order may not be made unless a place will be available at the hospital within 28 days.[68]

Accordingly, where the opinions of four psychiatrists were divided but the consultant at the state mental hospital was of the view that a person did not suffer from mental disorder and that a mental health disposal was not appropriate, the court held that the person had not been shown to be suffering from mental disorder and that no bed was available for him at the hospital.[69] A hospital order was therefore not granted.

5.9 Probation

5.9.1 General. A further option where a person is convicted in solemn proceedings of an offence (other than an offence the sentence for which is fixed by law), is that the court may, instead of sentencing him, make a probation order. It may do so where it is of the opinion, having regard to the circumstances including the nature of the offence and the character of the offender and having obtained a social enquiry report, that it was expedient to do so. A probation order is an order requiring the offender to be under supervision for a period of not less than six months nor more than three years.[70]

A summary court has a similar power which is exercised where the court is satisfied that the person committed the offence but without proceeding to conviction.[71] As a summary court when granting an absolute discharge does not proceed to conviction, it is not possible in such a case to appeal against conviction.[72] However, s. 392(4) of the 1975 Act now gives the same right of appeal against a finding leading to an absolute discharge as against conviction. If sentence had previously been deferred, there would be a conviction but this is not a bar to imposing a probation order.[73]

Before making a probation order a court should explain to the offender in ordinary language the effect of the order and that if he fails to comply with it or commits another offence during the probation period he will be liable to be convicted of and sentenced for the original offence. The court should not make the order unless the offender expresses his willingness to comply with the order's requirements.[74]

5.9.2 Contents of the order. The probation order should name the local authority area in which the offender resides or is to reside. It should make provision for the offender to be under the supervision of an officer of the local authority of that area. Where the offender resides or is to reside in a local authority area in which the court has no jurisdiction, the appropriate court in the area of residence or intended residence should be named. The appropriate court should require the local authority for that area to arrange for the offender to be under the supervision of an officer of that authority.[75]

A copy of the probation order should be given by the clerk of the court making the order or of the appropriate court to the supervising officer, to the probationer and to the person in charge of any institution or place in which the probationer is required to reside under the probation order.[76]

5.9.3 Additional requirements. A probation order may direct the offender to comply with such requirements as the court having regard to the circumstances of the case considers either necessary for securing the good conduct of the offender or for preventing a repetition by him of the offence or the commission of other offences, or conducive to the imposition of a community service or compensation requirement.[77]

A probation order may include requirements relating to the residence of the offender, but only where the court has first considered the home surroundings of the offender. If the order requires the offender to reside in any institution or place, the name of the institution or place and the period for which he is so required to reside there must be specified in the order. The period cannot extend beyond 12 months from the date of the requirement or beyond the expiry of the order.[78]

5.9.4 Probation and community service. In those areas where a scheme has been set up, a court may combine a probation order with community service if the offender is of or over 16 years of age, has committed an offence punishable with imprisonment and the conditions for making a community service order have been met.[79]

5.9.5 Probation and compensation order. In making a probation order a court may include a requirement that the offender shall pay compensation for any personal injury, loss or damage caused (whether directly or indirectly) by the acts which constituted the offence.[80]

In such a case, it should be a condition of the probation order that payment of the compensation be completed not more than 18 months after the making of the order or not later than two months before the end of the period of probation, whichever first occurs. The court has power to vary the terms of the requirement on the application of the offender or the supervising officer as a result of any change in the circumstances of the offender.[81]

5.9.6 Probation and forfeiture. As a forfeiture order proceeds upon a conviction,[82] forfeiture is not an appropriate disposal along with probation in a summary case. However, one may be made in relation to tools found in possession of a convicted thief that were used or intended for use in the commission of theft.[83]

5.9.7 Probation and imprisonment. A probation order and a sentence of imprisonment are wholly inconsistent and cannot stand together. A court cannot impose one on some charges on the complaint or indictment and the other on further charges. In one case where both had been imposed, it was the sentence of imprisonment which was quashed.[84]

5.9.8   Probation and security. When making a probation order a court may, if it deems such a course expedient, require the offender to give security for his good behaviour. Security may be given by consignation with the clerk of court or by entering into an undertaking to pay the amount, but not otherwise. The security may be forfeited and recovered in the same way as caution.[85]

5.9.9   Probation and deferred sentence. It is competent to make a probation order after sentence has been deferred, although the court would first have proceeded to conviction.[86]

5.9.10   Probation orders requiring treatment for mental condition. Where the court is satisfied, on the evidence of a registered medical practitioner approved for the purposes of ss. 20 or 39 of the Mental Health (Scotland) Act 1984 that the mental condition of an offender is such as requires and may be susceptible to treatment but is not such as to warrant his detention in pursuance of a hospital order, the court may if it makes a probation order include a requirement that the offender shall submit to treatment by or under the direction of a registered medical practitioner with a view to the improvement of the offender's mental condition. The requirement may not extend for more than 12 months.[87]

This provision does not mean that the determination of sentence is taken out of the hands of the court and left to the decision of either a probation officer or a psychiatrist. Their views are only facets of the problem which the court has to determine.[88]

5.9.11   Effects of order. A conviction for an offence for which an offender is placed on probation is deemed not to be a conviction for any purpose other than the purposes of the proceedings in which the order was made and of laying it before a court as a previous conviction in a subsequent case.[89]

Such a conviction is disregarded for the purposes of any enactment which imposes disqualification or disability upon convicted persons or authorises or requires the imposition of such disqualification or disability.[90] Formerly, unless there were special reasons it was not competent to order probation where an offence carried obligatory disqualification.[91] Otherwise, by imposing probation and thereby not proceeding to conviction the court effectively circumvented the obligatory disqualification provisions. However, it is now competent to combine probation with disqualification.[92]

Where a person has previously been placed on probation it is competent in subsequent proceedings to bring the probation order before the court in the same way as if the order were a conviction.[93]

5.9.12 Discharge and amendment of probation orders. Schedule 5 of the 1975 Act contains provision for the discharge and amendment of probation orders.[94]

5.9.13 Breach of probation order. Acting on information on oath from the supervising officer that the probationer has failed to comply with any of the requirements of the order, the court imposing the probation order or the appropriate court may issue a warrant for the arrest of the probationer or may issue a citation requiring the probationer to appear before the court.[95]

If it is proved to the satisfaction of the court that the probationer has failed to comply with any of the requirements of the probation order, the court may impose a fine not exceeding level 3 on the standard scale. However, a court may not do so in respect of a failure to comply with a requirement to pay compensation. Alternatively, it may sentence the offender as if he had not been placed on probation, convicting him first if he has not been convicted, vary the requirements of the order or, without prejudice to the continuance in force of the probation order, impose community service.[96]

It has been held in the sheriff court that where it is necessary to establish the fact that a breach of probation has occurred, the standard of proof is that appropriate to criminal proceedings, that is, proof beyond reasonable doubt by corroborated evidence. It was also observed that a notice of penalty should be served, although this has been doubted.[97]

The probationer may be sentenced for the original offence, first being convicted of it if that has not already happened.[98] The probation order will then cease to exist.[99] Any of the requirements of the probation order may be varied. However, any extension of the probation order must terminate not later than three years from the date of the probation order.[100]

5.9.14 Commission of further offence. There are two situations in which the commission of a further offence may alter a probation order. If the probationer is convicted by the court responsible for the probation order of an offence committed during the probation period, that court may if it thinks fit deal with him for both offences.[101]

If the probationer is convicted by a court in any part of Great Britain of an offence committed during the probation period and has been dealt with for that offence, the court responsible for the probation order may issue a warrant for his arrest or issue a citation requiring him to appear before that court. On his appearance, the court may if it thinks fit deal with him for the original offence.[102]

5.9.15 Reciprocal enforcement of probation orders. Arrangements have been made for the reciprocal enforcement of probation orders within the United Kingdom.[103]

5.9.16 Probation reports. A copy of any report by an officer of a local authority which is made to the court with a view to assisting the court in determining the most suitable method of dealing with the offender must be given by the clerk of the court to the offender or his solicitor. If the offender is under 16 years of age and is not represented by counsel or a solicitor, a copy of the report need not be given to him but must be given to his parent or guardian if present in court.[104]

5.10 Reference to reporter

5.10.1 Offences committed against a child. Any court by or before which a person is convicted of having committed certain offences may refer the child against whom the offence has been committed or any child who is or is likely to become a member of the same household as the person who has committed the offence to the reporter of the local authority in whose area the child resides. Those offences are any offence under s. 21 of the Children and Young Persons (Scotland) Act 1937, contained in Sch. 1 to the 1975 Act or in respect of a female person aged 17 years or over which constitutes the crime of incest. The court may also certify that the offence is a ground established for the purposes of Part III of the Social Work (Scotland) Act 1968.[105]

5.10.2 Reference to children's hearings. Where a child who is not subject to a supervision requirement pleads guilty to or is found guilty of an offence, the court may, instead of making an order or finding, remit the case to the reporter to arrange for its disposal by a children's hearing. Alternatively, the court may request the reporter to arrange a children's hearing for the purpose of obtaining their advice as to the treatment of the child.[106] In the latter case, after considering the advice of the children's hearing, the court may dispose of the case itself or remit it to the hearing for disposal.[107]

If a child who is subject to a supervision requirement pleads guilty to or is found guilty of an offence, the High Court of Justiciary may and the sheriff court must request the reporter to arrange a children's hearing to obtain their advice as to the treatment of the child. On consideration of that advice, the court may itself dispose of the case or remit it to a children's hearing for disposal.[108] Once a court has remitted a case to the reporter, the court's jurisdiction in respect of the case ceases.[109] These provisions do not apply in respect of an offence the sentence for which is fixed, as in the case of murder.[110]

A person over the age of 16 and less than 17½ not the subject of a supervision requirement who pleads guilty to or is found guilty of an offence in summary proceedings may be referred to the reporter. The reporter will arrange a children's hearing to obtain their advice as to the treatment of that person. On consideration of that advice the court may dispose of the case itself or, where the hearing have so advised, remit it to the reporter for disposal by a children's hearing.[111]

5.11 Suspended sentence

In response to a parliamentary question, the government has indicated that consideration is not being given to the introduction of suspended sentences in Scotland.[112] The report of the Review Committee on Parole and Related Issues in Scotland, published in March 1989, concluded that a suspended sentence would have no advantages over a deferred sentence and that it should not be introduced into Scots law.[113]

Notes

1. 1975 Act, s. 182.
2. 1975 Act, s. 383.
3. *Walker* v. *MacGillivray* (1980) S.C.C.R. Supp. 244.
4. 1975 Act, s. 436 as substituted by the 1980 Act, Sch. 7.
5. 1975 Act, ss. 191(1) and 392(1) as amended by the 1980 Act, Sch. 8.
6. See *Galloway* v. *Mackenzie* 1991 S.C.C.R. 548.
7. 1975 Act, ss. 191(2) and 392(2).
8. Road Traffic Offenders Act 1988, s. 46(3).
9. Licensed Premises (Exclusion of Certain Persons) Act 1980, s. 1.
10. Immigration Act 1971, ss. 3(6) and 6 as amended by the British Nationality Act 1981, Sch. 4 para. 2.
11. Civic Government (Scotland) Act 1982, s. 58(3).
12. 1975 Act, ss. 191(4) and 392(5).
13. 1975 Act, ss. 181 and 382.
14. *Non-custodial and Semi-custodial Penalties*, Advisory Council on the Penal System, 1970, H.M.S.O. See also D. Kelly, "Community Service", 1991 *Scottish Law Gazette* 47.
15. Herein referred to as the "1978 Act".
16. *Sentencers' Perceptions of Community Service by Offenders*, Scottish Office, Central Research Unit Papers, Nov. 1990, herein referred to as the "CRU Paper".
17. CRU Paper, p. 12.
18. 1988 S.C.C.R. 235.
19. 1978 Act, s. 1(7); 1980 Act, s. 58(1).
20. 1978 Act, s. 1(2)(c) and (d).
21. 1978 Act, s. 1(2)(a) and (4). The procedure for carrying out the order is set out in s. 3.
22. 1978 Act, ss. 1(1) and 2(2).
23. Criminal Justice Act 1991 s. 16 and Sch. 3.
24. 1986 S.C.C.R. 20.
25. *McLean* v. *H.M. Advocate* 1992 S.C.C.R. 755.
26. CRU Paper, p. 24.
27. 1978 Act, s. 5.
28. 1978 Act, s. 3(2).
29. 1978 Act, s. 5(1) and (3).
30. 1978 Act, s. 5(2).
31. 1987 S.C.C.R. 63.
32. 1978 Act, s. 4(1).
33. 1978 Act, s. 4(2) as amended by the Criminal Justice Act 1982, s. 56(3), Sch. 7 para. 12.
34. *O'Brien* v. *Dowdells* 1991 S.C.C.R. 912 (Sh. Ct.).
35. 1990 S.C.C.R. 524.
36. 1990 S.C.C.R. 607.
37. 1990 S.C.C.R. 680.
38. About half of those in the CRU Paper survey: at p. 15.
39. 1978 Act, s. 1(1).
40. 1978 Act, s. 1(5).
41. CRU Paper, p. 37.
42. 1988 S.C.C.R. 229.
43. CRU Paper, p. 42.
44. CRU Paper, pp. 51–52.

45. 1975 Act, s. 284.
46. CRU Paper, p. 55.
47. Murder (Abolition of Death Penalty) Act 1965; 1975 Act, s. 220.
48. Act of Adjournal (Consolidation) 1988, rule 75; Sch. 1, Form 34.
49. 1975 Act, ss. 219 and 432 as amended by the 1980 Act, ss. 53(2) and 54. See further A. D. Smith, "Deferred Sentence in Scotland", 1968 S.L.T. 153.
50. *H.M. Advocate* v. *Clegg* 1990 J.C. 318; 1990 S.C.C.R. 293; 1991 S.L.T. 192; *Wilson* v. *Donald* 1992 S.C.C.R. 654.
51. *Young* v. *McGlennan* 1990 S.C.C.R. 373; 1991 S.L.T. 375.
52. *Lennon* v. *Copeland* 1972 S.L.T. (Notes) 68.
53. *McPherson* v. *H.M. Advocate* 1986 S.C.C.R. 278.
54. *Cassidy* v. *Wilson* 1989 S.C.C.R. 6.
55. *Colquhoun* v. *H.M. Advocate* 1985 S.C.C.R. 396.
56. *Linton* v. *Ingram* 1989 S.C.C.R. 487.
57. *Maxwell* v. *MacPhail* 1990 S.C.C.R. 738.
58. *Islam* v. *H.M. Advocate* 1989 S.C.C.R. 109; *Main* v. *Jessop* 1989 S.C.C.R. 437; *Beattie* v. *McGlennan* 1990 S.C.C.R. 497; 1991 S.L.T. 384.
59. Immigration Act 1971, ss. 3(6) and 6(3) as amended by the British Nationality Act 1981, s. 39(6), Sch. 4 para. 2 and the Criminal Justice Act 1982, s. 77, Sch. 15 para. 15.
60. *Willms* v. *Smith* 1982 J.C. 9; 1981 S.C.C.R. 257; 1982 S.L.T. 163, following *R.* v. *Nazari* [1980] 1 W.L.R. 1366; [1980] 3 All E.R. 880; 71 Cr. App. R. 87; *H.M. Advocate* v. *Riganti* 1992 S.C.C.R. 891. On the special position of European Community nationals, see also Renton and Brown's *Criminal Procedure* (5th edn.), para. 17–87.
61. *Faboro* v. *H.M. Advocate* 1982 S.C.C.R. 22.
62. *Caldewei* v. *Jessop* 1991 S.C.C.R. 323.
63. *Salehi* v. *Smith* 1982 S.C.C.R. 552.
64. 1975 Act, ss. 175 and 376 as amended by the Mental Health (Amendment) (Scotland) Act 1983, Sch. 2 paras. 31 and 34 and amended by the Mental Health (Scotland) Act 1984, Sch. 3 paras. 26 and 33.
65. 1975 Act, ss. 175 and 376.
66. 1975 Act, ss. 174A and 375A as inserted by the Mental Health (Amendment) (Scotland) Act 1983, s. 34 and amended by the Mental Health (Scotland) Act 1984, Sch. 3 paras. 25 and 32.
67. 1975 Act, ss. 175(1) and 376(1). See also ss. 176–178 and 377–379.
68. 1975 Act, ss. 175(3) and 376(6).
69. *Allan* v. *H.M. Advocate* 1983 S.C.C.R. 183.
70. 1975 Act, s. 183(1). On the use made of probation orders, see G. Moore and C. Wood, "The Power of Positive Sentencing", 1988 S.L.T. 52.
71. 1975 Act, s. 384(1) as amended by the Criminal Justice (Scotland) Act 1987, s. 65, Sch. 1 para. 10.
72. *Cf. Walker* v. *MacGillivray* (1980) S.C.C.R. Supp. 244.
73. 1975 Act, ss. 384(1) and 432 as amended by the 1980 Act, ss. 53 and 54.
74. 1975 Act, ss. 183(6) and 384(6) as amended by the Community Service by Offenders (Scotland) Act 1978, s. 7 and the Criminal Justice Act 1982, s. 68(2), Sch. 13 para. 3.
75. 1975 Act, ss. 183(2) and 384(2). For the form of order, see Act of Adjournal (Consolidation) 1988, rr. 76, 126, Sch. 1, Form 36.
76. 1975 Act, ss. 183(7) and 384(7).
77. 1975 Act, ss. 183(4) and 384(4) as amended by the Community Service by Offenders (Scotland) Act 1978, s. 7.

78. 1975 Act, ss. 183(5) and 384(5).
79. 1975 Act, ss. 183(5A) and 384(5A) as added by the Community Service by Offenders (Scotland) Act 1978, s. 7 and amended by the Criminal Justice Act 1982, Sch. 13 para. 3.
80. 1975 Act, ss. 183(5B) and 384(5B) as added by the Criminal Justice (Scotland) Act 1987, s. 65.
81. 1975 Act, ss. 183(5C) and 384(5C).
82. 1975 Act, s. 436.
83. Civic Government (Scotland) Act 1982, s. 58(3).
84. *Dowie* v. *Irvine* 1964 J.C. 52; 1964 S.L.T. 205.
85. 1975 Act, ss. 190 and 391.
86. 1980 Act, s. 53, amending ss. 384(1) and 432 of the 1975 Act.
87. 1975 Act, ss. 184 and 385 as amended by the Mental Health (Amendment) (Scotland) Act 1983, s. 36, Sch. 3 and the Mental Health (Scotland) Act 1984, s. 127(1), Sch. 3 paras. 29 and 36.
88. *Isaacs* v. *H.M. Advocate* 1963 J.C. 71.
89. 1975 Act, ss. 191(1) and 392(1) as amended by the 1980 Act, Sch. 8.
90. 1975 Act, ss. 191(2) and 392(2).
91. *Herron* v. *Kent* (1976) S.C.C.R. Supp. 147; *Dennis* v. *Tame* [1954] 1 W.L.R. 1338n relied upon. *Cf. McPherson* v. *Henderson* 1984 S.C.C.R. 294.
92. Road Traffic Offenders Act 1988, s. 46(3).
93. 1975 Act, ss. 191(4) and 392(5), *Johnston* v. *Heatly* 1960 J.C. 26; 1960 S.L.T. 342.
94. 1975 Act, ss. 185 and 386.
95. 1975 Act, ss. 186(1) and 387(1) as amended by the 1980 Act, s. 46.
96. 1975 Act, ss. 186(2) and 387(2) as amended by the Community Service by Offenders (Scotland) Act 1978, s. 8, the Criminal Justice (Scotland) Act 1980, s. 46(1), the Criminal Justice Act 1982, s. 56(3), Sch. 7, paras. 3 and 9 and the Criminal Justice (Scotland) Act 1987, s. 65(5).
97. *Valentine* v. *Kennedy* 1987 S.C.C.R. 47 (Sh. Ct.) and Commentary thereon.
98. 1975 Act, ss. 186(2)(b) and 387(2)(b).
99. 1975 Act, ss. 185(2) and 386(2).
100. 1975 Act, ss. 186(2)(c) and 387(2)(c).
101. 1975 Act, ss. 187(2) and 388(2).
102. 1975 Act, ss. 187(1) and 388(1). *Cf. Roy* v. *Cruickshank* 1954 S.L.T. 217.
103. Criminal Justice Act 1991, s. 16 and Sch. 3.
104. 1975 Act, ss. 192 and 393.
105. 1975 Act, ss. 168 and 364 as amended by the 1980 Act, Sch. 7.
106. 1975 Act, ss. 173(1) and 372(1). (S. 173 was amended by the 1980 Act, Sch. 7 para. 35.)
107. 1975 Act, ss. 173(2) and 372(2).
108. 1975 Act, ss. 173(3) and 372(3).
109. 1975 Act, ss. 173(4) and 372(4).
110. 1975 Act, ss. 173(5) and 372(5).
111. 1975 Act, s. 373.
112. H.L. Hansard, Vol. 524, c. 46, 18/12/90.
113. Cm. 598.

CHAPTER 6

FINES AND FINANCIAL ORDERS

6.1 Fine

6.1.1 European Court of Justice. The powers of the European institutions to enforce Community law should not be over-looked, not least because of the size of the fines which have amounted to several million pounds. However, the enforcement of Community law is outwith the scope of this work, which concentrates on the decisions of the Scottish courts.

6.1.2 Fine on conviction on indictment. A person convicted on indictment of any offence, is liable to a fine of any amount, even where the statute fixes an amount or a minimum amount.[1] This also applies where an Act confers a power by subordinate instrument to make a person liable on conviction on indictment of an offence to a fine or to a maximum fine of a specified amount.[2] However, there is an exception if the offence could be tried only summarily and has been included by virtue of s.457A(4) of the 1975 Act.

6.1.3 Fine by sheriff sitting summarily. A sheriff has power on convicting a person of a common law offence to impose a fine not exceeding the prescribed sum within the meaning of s.289B of the 1975 Act, currently £5,000.[3]

6.1.4 Fine by district court. The district court is entitled on conviction of a common law offence to impose a fine not exceeding level 4 on the standard scale, currently £2,500.[4]

6.1.5 The standard scale. There is a standard scale of fines for offences triable only summarily. It is as follows:

Standard Scale	*Level*	*Amount*
	1	£200
	2	£500
	3	£1,000
	4	£2,500
	5	£5,000.[5]

6.1.6 Fine in addition to maximum term of imprisonment.
Imprisonment in default of payment of a fine, if that did in fact
arise at a later stage when the fine was not paid, would be
imprisonment for failure to pay it and not for a contravention of
the original offence. A fine in addition to a maximum period of
imprisonment for an offence is competent. However, where the
additional period of imprisonment exceeded the statutory
maximum powers of a summary court, it was suspended.[6]

6.1.7 Means of the offender. In determining the amount of
any fine, a court should take into consideration, amongst other
things, the means of the offender so far as known to the court.[7]
If the result of the fine imposed would be that the offender could
not pay it or the instalments set and would therefore almost
certainly find himself in prison for non-payment, the fine would
be considered excessive.[8] A £500 fine for breach of the peace by
someone earning £76 net per week was not considered to be
excessive.[9]

However, even if an offender has meagre resources it may be
necessary to impose fines in order to mark the offences, leaving
the matter to a means enquiry court if he finds it impossible to
pay them.[10]

When sentencing co-accused for an offence, in assessing any
fines imposed the courts should have close regard to differences
in their incomes. Where four co-accused were equally blame-
worthy of an offence and the sheriff determined that the penalty
for each should be a fine representing five weeks' income, the
Court of Criminal Appeal held that he had assessed the fines in
the correct manner.[11]

6.1.8 Place of enforcement. A fine imposed by a sheriff or
district court may be enforced against the person fined or his
effects in any other sheriff court district as well as the district
where it is imposed. If enforced in another district, an extract of
the fine must first be produced to and endorsed by the sheriff or
justice of the other district competent to have imposed such fine
in that district.[12]

A fine imposed by the High Court of Justiciary is remitted for
enforcement to the sheriff for the district where the offender
resides, where he resides in Scotland. Where he resides outwith
Scotland, it is remitted to the sheriff before whom he was

brought for examination in relation to the offence for which the fine was imposed.[13]

6.1.9 Remission of fines. A fine may at any time be remitted in whole or in part by the court which imposed the fine or, where that court was the High Court of Justiciary, the court by which payment was first enforceable. If a transfer of fine order is effective and the court by which payment is enforceable is a court of summary jurisdiction in Scotland, that court has the power to remit the fine.[14] The accused need not be present.[15]

If a court remits a fine after the alternative of imprisonment has been imposed, it must also remit the whole period of imprisonment or reduce it by the same proportion as the amount remitted bears to the whole fine.[16]

In imposing a fine the court should not have regard to its power to remit a fine and impose a high fine on the basis that the offender can subsequently seek to have it remitted.[17]

6.1.10 Time for payment. In imposing a fine or ordering the finding of caution a court must allow the offender at least seven days to pay the fine or the first instalment of it or to find the caution.[18] The court has power to allow time to pay even where that has not been requested by the offender.[19]

However, the court may refuse the offender time to pay if when imposing the fine, (1) it appears to the court that the offender possesses sufficient means to enable him to pay the fine forthwith; or (2) on being asked by the court whether he wishes to have time for payment, he does not ask for time; or (3) he fails to satisfy the court that he has a fixed abode; or (4) the court is satisfied for any other special reason that no time should be allowed for payment. The special reason must be stated.[20] If time is not allowed for payment of a fine, the reasons of the court for not so allowing time should be stated in the extract of the finding and sentence as well as in the finding and sentence itself.[21] If no time is allowed for payment and the offender fails to pay, the court may impose an alternative period of imprisonment.[22]

It has been held in relation to earlier legislation that the nature of the offence can never be a relevant consideration when determining whether time should be allowed for payment. The only relevant considerations are the means of the offender, his ability to make immediate payment and similar considerations. Where the offence is of such a grave character as to warrant the imposition of a term of imprisonment, the proper course is to impose such a sentence and not to purport to impose a fine but, by making it of such a large amount and by refusing time to pay, in effect converting it into a sentence of imprisonment.[23]

. The fact that a person is serving a sentence of imprisonment is not a special reason for refusing time to pay.[24]

6.1.11 Application for further time to pay. Where time has been allowed for payment of a fine, further time may be allowed for payment if applied for by or on behalf of the offender.[25] The prosecutor has the opportunity to be heard should he wish to be.

An application by an offender for further time to pay a fine adjudged to be paid by him by a court or instalments of it should be made to that court. However, if the fine has been transferred to another court, the application should be addressed to the court specified in the transfer order or the last transfer order if more than one.[26]

The application for further time to pay should be allowed by the court unless it is satisfied that the failure of the offender to make payment has been wilful or that the offender has no reasonable prospect of being able to pay if further time is allowed.[27] An application may be made either orally or in writing.[28]

6.1.12 Payment by instalments. Where a court has imposed a fine on an offender, it may of its own accord or on the application of the offender order payment of that fine by instalments of such amounts and at such time as it thinks fit. Further time may be allowed for payment of any instalment. Lower instalments or payment at longer intervals may be allowed. The offender need not be present.[29] There is no general rule that the fine imposed should not exceed the amount which an offender could be expected to pay by instalments within one year. A longer period may be required.[30]

6.1.13 Supervision pending payment of fine. The court may order that an offender who is allowed time for payment be placed under the supervision of someone appointed by it for the purpose of assisting and advising the offender in regard to payment of the fine.[31]

If the offender is under 21 years of age and has been allowed time for payment of the fine, the court may not order detention in default of payment unless he has first been placed under supervision in respect of the fine or the court is satisfied that it is impracticable to place him under supervision.[32] The court must state the grounds on which it is so satisfied.[33]

6.1.14 Alternative of imprisonment.

General. When imposing a fine a court may impose a period of imprisonment in default of payment. If no such order has been made and a person fails to pay a fine, or any part or instalment of it, by the time ordered by the court, or immediately if no time has been allowed for payment, the court may then impose a period of imprisonment for the failure.[34]

Where time is allowed for payment of a fine or payment by instalments is ordered, a court may not, on the occasion of the imposition of the fine, impose imprisonment in the event of a future default in paying the fine or an instalment of it unless the offender is before it and the court determines that, having regard to the gravity of the offence or to the character of the offender or to some other special reason, it was expedient that he should be imprisoned without further enquiry in default of payment. The court must state the special reason for its decision.[35] Where imprisonment is so imposed and the offender asks the court to commit him to prison, the court may do so.[36]

The nature of the offence is not a relevant reason for imposing the alternative.[37]

It is not competent to impose the alternative of imprisonment on the ground of the gravity of the offence for an offence for which imprisonment is not a competent disposal available to the court as a penalty for the commission of that offence. Otherwise, imprisonment of the offender, which was an incompetent penalty, could be secured by a court imposing a fine which was beyond the means of an offender to pay. Thus, careless driving, however grave, is not an offence of gravity within the meaning of s. 396(4) of the 1975 Act.[38] The mere fact that an offender has previous convictions is not in itself a special reason for imposing the alternative of imprisonment.[39]

At times it is considered appropriate to impose the alternative of imprisonment at the time of sentence. A first offender has been fined £100 for stealing a pair of boots by shoplifting where the special reason for imposing the alternative of 30 days' imprisonment in default was given as "the nature of the offence" which was "barefaced shoplifting". This was described by the appeal court as "the very case in which it was appropriate for the sheriff to take the course he did".[40]

In imposing the alternative of imprisonment on an offender who has not previously received a custodial disposal, it is not necessary first to obtain a social enquiry report since the court in fining the offender is dealing with him in a method other than by way of imprisonment.[41]

In the normal case where an application is made for extension of time to pay or the imposition of the alternative period of imprisonment and the offender is not serving another period of imprisonment at the time, it may well be that no hearing is necessary provided that the alternative of imprisonment to a fine has been imposed by the court when the fine was initially fixed. However, where the offender is serving a period of imprisonment at the time and an issue arises as to whether the alternative period of imprisonment should run concurrently or consecutively, the accused should be given the opportunity to be heard and any sentence imposed should be pronounced in open court in the presence of the accused.[42]

Imposed as a consecutive sentence. It has been held that the power to impose a consecutive sentence under s. 430(4) of the 1975 Act does not apply where a judge is imposing periods of detention in default of payment.[43] However, a court of summary jurisdiction has an inherent power at common law to impose consecutive sentences provided that the sentences in aggregate do not exceed the limit of the court's sentencing power. Thus, if a court is sentencing an accused to imprisonment on a complaint and at the same time is imposing imprisonment in default of payment of a fine, there is nothing in principle to prevent the court from ordering that the two periods of imprisonment should run consecutively.[44]

A court of five judges has now held that power to impose consecutive sentences is available at common law in all circumstances which merit this disposal unless there is some statutory provision precluding this.[45] In imposing imprisonment or detention for non-payment of a fine, it is generally accepted that a court may order that consecutive sentences should be served if it is dealing on the same day with the non-payment of fines imposed on different days or in different courts in respect of two or more separate complaints. This is based on the common law principle that a custodial sentence should be effective. It was considered to be a logical application of this principle that the court had power to order that a period of detention or imprisonment for non-payment of a fine should be served consecutively to a period of detention already being served for non-payment as a result of a previous order imposed at an earlier date.

Detention in different parts of the United Kingdom. A person aged 17 or over may be arrested in any part of the United Kingdom on the basis of an extract conviction issued in Scotland for imprisonment in default of a fine. In order to avoid the expense of returning him to the place of the fine, the defaulter may be imprisoned where arrested.[46]

Supervised attendance orders. In place of a period of imprisonment for non-payment of a fine, the court may order an adult offender to attend a place of supervision for between 10 and 60 hours.[47]

6.1.15 Period of imprisonment for non-payment of fine. The maximum period of imprisonment which may be imposed for failure to pay a fine or any part or instalment of it or for failure to find caution is as follows:

Amount of fine or caution	Maximum period of imprisonment
Not exceeding £200	7 days
Exceeding £200 but not exceeding £500	14 days
Exceeding £500 but not exceeding £1,000	28 days
Exceeding £1,000 but not exceeding £2,500	45 days
Exceeding £2,500 but not exceeding £5,000	3 months
Exceeding £5,000 but not exceeding £10,000	6 months
Exceeding £10,000 but not exceeding £20,000	12 months
Exceeding £20,000 but not exceeding £50,000	18 months
Exceeding £50,000 but not exceeding £100,000	2 years
Exceeding £100,000 but not exceeding £250,000	3 years
Exceeding £250,000 but not exceeding £1,000,000	5 years
Exceeding £1,000,000	10 years.[48]

If part only of the fine has not been paid, the offender is liable to imprisonment for the outstanding portion only.[49]

If a fine imposed by a summary court is paid at the bar it is not necessary for the court to refer to the period of imprisonment applicable had it not been paid.[50]

A sheriff may, if he considers that the imposition of three years' imprisonment would be inadequate and the maximum period which may be imposed in default is more than that, remit the case to the High Court of Justiciary for sentence.[51]

6.1.16 Payment of fine in part by prisoner. A person committed to prison or detained for failure to pay a fine may pay any sum in part satisfaction of that fine to the governor or officer in charge of the prison or place of detention. The term of imprisonment would then be reduced by the same proportion as the sum paid bore to the amount of the fine outstanding at the commencement of the imprisonment.[52]

6.1.17 Restrictions on imprisonment after fine or caution. Where a court has not imposed the alternative of imprisonment in default of payment when imposing a fine or ordering the finding of caution, it may not impose the alternative of imprisonment for failure to pay unless the court on a subsequent occasion enquires into the reason why the fine has not been paid in the presence of the offender. However, this does not apply if the offender is in prison.[53] An offender may be cited to a court for such enquiry to be made of him or may be brought under warrant.[54]

After the court has made such enquiry of the offender, it may not impose the alternative of imprisonment in the event of future default. That may only be done at the same time as the fine is imposed. The court at this stage can impose only immediate imprisonment.[55]

If a statute provides for a maximum prison sentence and a fine, the period specified will be the overriding maximum limit on the court's power to impose imprisonment. The court could not impose the maximum sentence and then in addition impose a further period as an alternative for non-payment of the fine.[56]

6.1.18 Transfer of fine orders. A court which has imposed a fine on a person convicted of an offence may order that payment of the fine shall be enforceable by the court where he is residing, if that is elsewhere in Scotland, in England or Wales or in Northern Ireland.[57]

6.1.19 Default by child. A court may order that a child who, if he were an adult, would be liable to be imprisoned in default of payment of a fine be detained for such period not exceeding one month in a place chosen by the local authority in whose area the court is situated.[58]

6.1.20 Recovery by civil diligence. A court may order a fine to be recovered by civil diligence. A warrant is added to the finding of the court imposing the fine authorising the charging of the person fined to pay the fine within a specified period and in the event of failure to do so, authorising the execution of an earnings or other type of arrestment and the poinding of articles belonging to him.[59]

6.2 Caution

A sheriff has power on convicting a person of a common law offence to ordain that person to find caution for good behaviour for any period not exceeding 12 months and to an amount not exceeding the prescribed sum, which is currently £5,000. The caution may be either in lieu of or in addition to a fine or in addition to imprisonment.[60] The district court on convicting of a common law offence is entitled to ordain the offender (in lieu of or in addition to imprisonment or fine) to find caution for good behaviour for any period not exceeding six months and to an amount not exceeding level 4 on the standard scale, currently £2,500.[61] It has been stated that there is presumably unlimited power to order caution on conviction of common law offences on indictment.[62]

The court may impose the finding of the same amount of caution on a statutory offence as the amount of any fine which could be imposed.[63] On failure to find the caution, the alternative of imprisonment may be imposed.[64] The provisions relating to the imposition of imprisonment for non-payment of fines apply equally to caution.[65]

In summary proceedings caution may be found by consignation of the amount with the clerk of court or by bond of caution. Where caution becomes liable to forfeiture, forfeiture may be

granted on the motion of the prosecutor. In the event of a
cautioner failing to pay the amount due under his bond within
six days of receiving a charge to that effect, the alternative of
imprisonment may be imposed, time may be granted for
payment or recovery by civil diligence may be ordered.[66]

6.3 Compensation order

6.3.1 General. Following the Dunpark Report, a general
system of compensation administered by the criminal courts
was introduced into Scotland.[67] Where a person is convicted of
an offence the court, instead of or in addition to dealing with
him in any other way, may make an order requiring him to pay
compensation for any personal injury, loss or damage caused
(whether directly or indirectly) by the acts which constituted the
offence.[68] A compensation order may not be made to a person
solely because he was terrified or alarmed by an offence.
Compensation orders to passengers of a car involved in a breach
of the peace who were placed in a state of fear and alarm were
quashed because there was no evidence of any personal injury,
loss or damage to them.[69]

It is not competent for a court to make a compensation order
where it discharges the offender absolutely or at the same time
as deferring sentence.[70] In the case of an offence involving the
dishonest appropriation, or the unlawful taking and using, of
property including of a motor vehicle, if the property is
recovered but has been damaged while out of the owner's
possession, that damage (however and by whomsoever caused)
is treated as having been caused by the acts which constituted
the offence.[71] No compensation order may be made in respect of
loss suffered in consequence of the death of any person or of
injury, loss or damage due to a road accident apart from in
taking and driving away a vehicle.[72]

A compensation order is paid to the clerk of court who accounts
for it to the recipient of it. Only the court has power to enforce the
order.[73] If the offender has insufficient means to pay both a fine
and a compensation order but both would be appropriate, the
court should prefer a compensation order.[74] Where both are
imposed, a payment made by the offender will first be applied in
satisfaction of the compensation order.[75] In general the compensation order is enforced in the same way as a fine.[76]

6.3.2 Amount of compensation orders. There is no limit to the amount of a compensation order in solemn proceedings. In summary proceedings the limit in the sheriff court is the prescribed sum and in the district court is level 4 on the standard scale. The means of the offender is to be taken into account in determining whether to make a compensation order and the amount of the order. However, if the person is serving or is about to serve a custodial sentence no account is to be taken of earnings contingent upon his obtaining employment after his release.[77]

6.3.3 Variation and reduction of compensation orders. At any time before a compensation order is fully complied with, the court may vary the terms of the order. A variation may be made in chambers and in the absence of the parties. The court may dispose of an application to discharge a compensation order or to reduce the amount remaining unpaid which has been made in writing to the clerk of court and intimated to the prosecutor.[78]

6.3.4 Practice. For a court to impose a compensation order, the loss to the victim does not require to be established by corroborated evidence.[79]

In circumstances where a compensation order has been made to someone who unbeknown to the court had died, a sheriff has held that the fact that the person was dead did not invalidate the order. At a subsequent diet he directed the sheriff clerk to pay the compensation to the deceased person's insurance brokers, the insurance company having borne the loss.[80]

The amount of the compensation order need not be restricted to the amount of any actual damage done. A compensation order for £500 has been upheld where a car valued at £400 was stolen and written off, the additional £100 being in respect of inconvenience suffered by the owner.[81] A compensation order for £125 to the householder in payment for the cost of repairing the damage to her house and for the distress and humiliation inevitably accompanying a housebreaking, which was imposed in addition to a sentence of four months' imprisonment, has been upheld, although earlier cases on awarding compensation for distress and humiliation were not referred to.[82]

It has been held in the sheriff court that a compensation order is not restricted to those cases where the legal position was clear and bereft of complexities and the damage was capable of precise valuation and was not great. A compensation order for £1,000 was imposed on a shopkeeper who sold fireworks to 11-year-old boys, one of whom was later injured by them.[83]

If the circumstances of an offence are such that the victim would not recover compensation from the Criminal Injuries Compensation Board, it would not be appropriate for him to receive compensation by a court order.[84] A compensation order imposed in addition to the maximum sentence of imprisonment within the court's powers was considered to be excessive and was quashed.[85] A compensation order which would have taken over four years to pay by instalments was quashed in that it would be unreasonable to expect the offender to continue making payment by way of compensation over such a long period.[86]

6.4 Fixed penalty

As an alternative to prosecution certain minor road traffic cases are dealt with by the conditional offer of an opportunity to pay a fixed penalty and to have any obligatory penalty points endorsed on the person's licence.[87] If payment is made in time and all other conditions are complied with no criminal proceedings may be brought for the offence.

A system is also in operation in respect of other minor cases and again if the "fiscal fine" is paid in time no criminal proceedings may follow.[88]

Notes

1. 1975 Act, s. 193A(1). (S. 193A was added by the Criminal Law Act 1977, s. 63(1), Sch. 11 para. 1 and amended by the 1980 Act, s. 83(2), Sch. 7 para. 37 and the Criminal Justice Act 1982, s. 77, Sch. 15 para. 17.)
2. 1975 Act, s. 193A(2).
3. 1975 Act, s. 289(a) as amended by the Criminal Law Act 1977, Sch. 11 para. 4, and the Criminal Justice Act 1991, s. 17(2).
4. 1975 Act, ss. 284(b) (as amended by the Criminal Law Act 1977, Sch. 11 para. 3, and the Criminal Justice Act 1982, s. 56(3), Sch. 7 para. 4) and 289G (as added by the Criminal Justice Act 1982, s. 54 and amended by the Increase of Penalties etc. (Scotland) Order, art. 4).
5. 1975 Act, s. 289G, as amended by the Criminal Justice Act 1991, s. 17(1).
6. *Fraser* v. *Herron* 1968 J.C. 1; 1968 S.L.T. 149; *Beattie* v. *H.M. Advocate* 1986 S.C.C.R. 605. *Cf. Beattie, Ptnr* 1992 S.C.C.R. 812.
7. 1975 Act, ss. 194 and 395(1) as amended by the 1980 Act, Sch. 7 para. 60. Section 194 was substituted by the 1980 Act, s. 47. *Brown* v. *Carmichael* 1987 S.C.C.R. 183. See R. Black, "Fine Tuning", 1986 S.L.T. 185.

8. *Hamilton* v. *Scott* 1987 S.C.C.R. 188.
9. *Thomson* v. *Allan* 1987 S.C.C.R. 201.
10. *Buchan* v. *McNaughtan* 1990 S.C.C.R. 13.
11. *Scott* v. *Lowe* 1990 S.C.C.R. 15.
12. 1975 Act, ss. 196(1) and 402.
13. 1975 Act, s. 196(2) as inserted by the 1980 Act, s. 48.
14. 1975 Act, ss. 194 and 395A(1). Section 395A was inserted by the 1980 Act, s. 49.
15. 1975 Act, ss. 194 and 395A(3).
16. 1975 Act, ss. 194 and 395A(2).
17. *McCandless* v. *MacDougall* 1987 S.C.C.R. 206.
18. 1975 Act, ss. 194 and 396(1).
19. *Fraser* v. *Herron* 1968 J.C. 1; 1968 S.L.T. 149.
20. 1975 Act, ss. 194 and 396(2).
21. 1975 Act, ss. 194 and 396(3).
22. 1975 Act, ss. 194 and 396(1).
23. *Barbour* v. *Robertson; Ram* v. *Robertson* 1943 J.C. 46.
24. *Robertson* v. *Jessop* 1989 S.C.C.R. 387; 1989 S.L.T. 843.
25. 1975 Act, ss. 194 and 396(7).
26. 1975 Act, ss. 194 and 397(1). S. 397 was amended by the Criminal Law Act 1977, Sch. 11 para. 8.
27. 1975 Act, ss. 194 and 397(2).
28. 1975 Act, ss. 194 and 397(3).
29. 1975 Act, ss. 194 and 399 as amended by the 1980 Act, s. 83, Sch. 7 para. 62, Sch. 8.
30. *Johnston* v. *Lockhart* 1987 S.C.C.R. 337; *Glen* v. *McLeod* 1982 S.C.C.R. 449.
31. 1975 Act, ss. 194 and 400(1).
32. 1975 Act, ss. 194 and 400(4).
33. 1975 Act, ss. 194 and 400(5).
34. 1975 Act, ss. 194 and 407(1) as substituted by the 1980 Act, s. 50, Sch. 6 para. 3.
35. 1975 Act, ss. 194 and 396(4).
36. 1975 Act, ss. 194 and 396(5).
37. *Buchanan* v. *Hamilton* 1988 S.C.C.R. 379.
38. *Dunlop* v. *Allan* 1984 S.C.C.R. 329.
39. *Paterson* v. *McGlennan* 1991 S.C.C.R. 616; 1991 S.L.T. 832.
40. *Finnie* v. *McLeod* 1983 S.C.C.R. 387, 388.
41. *Sullivan* v. *McLeod* 1980 S.L.T. (Notes) 99.
42. 1975 Act, s. 433; *Campbell* v. *Jessop* 1987 S.C.C.R. 670; 1988 S.L.T. 160; *Nash, Petitioner* 1991 S.C.C.R. 978; 1992 S.L.T. 147.
43. *Cartledge* v. *McLeod* 1988 S.C.C.R. 129; 1988 S.L.T. 389; *Cain* v. *Carmichael* 1990 S.C.C.R. 369; 1991 S.L.T. 442.
44. *Young* v. *McGlennan* 1990 S.C.C.R. 373. See also *Beattie* v. *McGlennan* 1990 S.C.C.R. 497; 1991 S.L.T. 384.
45. *Russell* v. *MacPhail* 1990 J.C. 380; 1990 S.C.C.R. 628; 1991 S.L.T. 449.
46. Criminal Law Act 1977, s. 38A(1) and (3) as added by the 1980 Act, s. 51 and amended by the Criminal Justice Act 1982, s. 77, Sch. 14 para. 39.
47. Law Reform (Miscellaneous Provisions) (Scotland) Act 1990, s. 62.
48. 1975 Act, ss. 194 and 407(1A) as added by the 1980 Act, s. 50 and amended by the Increase of Penalties etc. (Scotland) Order 1984, art. 5, the Law Reform (Miscellaneous Provisions) (Scotland) Act 1985, s. 40, the Criminal Justice (Scotland) Act 1987, s. 67, and the Criminal Justice Act 1991, s. 23(2).
49. 1975 Act, ss. 194 and 407(1C).

50. 1975 Act, s. 430(2).
51. 1975 Act, ss. 194 and 407(5).
52. 1975 Act, ss. 194 and 409 as amended by the 1980 Act, Sch. 7.
53. 1975 Act, ss. 194 and 398(1) as amended by the 1980 Act, Sch. 7 para. 61.
54. 1975 Act, ss. 194 and 398(2)–(4).
55. 1975 Act, s. 407(1); *Craig* v. *Smith* 1990 S.C.C.R. 328.
56. *Fraser* v. *Herron* 1968 J.C. 1; 1968 S.L.T. 149.
57. 1975 Act, ss. 194, 403 and 404.
58. 1975 Act, ss. 194 and 406.
59. 1975 Act, ss. 194 and 411 as amended by the 1980 Act, s. 52, Sch. 7 para. 66, Sch. 8.
60. 1975 Act, ss. 289(b) (as amended by the Criminal Law Act 1977, Sch. 11 para. 4) and 289B (as added by the Criminal Law Act 1977, Sch. 11 para. 5 and substituted by the Criminal Justice Act 1982, s. 55).
61. 1975 Act, ss. 284(c) and 289G as added by the Criminal Justice Act 1982, s. 54, and amended by the Criminal Justice Act 1991, s. 17(2).
62. Renton and Brown's *Criminal Procedure* (5th edn.), para. 17–37.
63. 1975 Act, ss. 193(3) and 394(c).
64. 1975 Act, ss. 284(d) and 289(c).
65. See para. 6.1 for the procedure adopted and the periods of imprisonment.
66. 1975 Act, s. 303(1).
67. *Report of Committee on Reparation by the Victim to the Offender in Scotland*, Cmnd. 6802 (1977).
68. 1980 Act, s. 58(1). For the terms of the order, see Act of Adjournal (Consolidation) 1988, rules 78 and 125. For the effect of the order on a subsequent award of damages, see the 1980 Act, s. 67.
69. *Smillie* v. *Wilson* 1990 S.C.C.R. 133. On factors which may be taken into account in assessing compensation, see *Robertson* v. *Lees* 1992 S.C.C.R. 545.
70. 1980 Act, s. 58(1).
71. 1980 Act, s. 58(2).
72. 1980 Act, s. 58(3).
73. 1980 Act, s. 60.
74. 1980 Act, s. 61.
75. 1980 Act. s. 62.
76. 1980 Act, s. 66, which applies the fines enforcement procedure with the exception of the power to impose imprisonment for default at the same time as the imposition of a fine.
77. 1980 Act, s. 59 as amended by the Criminal Justice Act 1982, s. 56(3), Sch. 7 para. 16. *Cf. Notman* v. *Henderson* 1992 S.C.C.R. 409.
78. Act of Adjournal (Consolidation) 1988, rules 80, 81 and 125.
79. *Goodhall* v. *Carmichael* 1984 S.C.C.R. 247. For a critique of this case, see C. J. Docherty and G. Maher, "Corroboration and Compensation Orders", 1984 S.L.T. 125.
80. *Tudhope* v. *Furphy* 1982 S.C.C.R. 575 (Sh. Ct.); 1984 S.L.T. (Sh. Ct.) 33.
81. *Stewart* v. *H.M. Advocate* 1982 S.C.C.R. 203.
82. *Collins* v. *Lowe* 1990 S.C.C.R. 605.
83. *Carmichael* v. *Siddique* 1985 S.C.C.R. 145 (Sh. Ct.).
84. *Brown* v. *Normand* 1988 S.C.C.R. 229.
85. *Clark* v. *Cardle* 1989 S.C.C.R. 92.
86. *Storie* v. *Scott* 1990 S.C.C.R. 284.
87. Road Traffic Offenders Act 1988, ss. 75–78, as amended by the Road Traffic Act 1991, s. 34.
88. Criminal Justice (Scotland) Act 1987, s. 56.

CHAPTER 7

FORFEITURE AND CONFISCATION

7.1 Forfeiture

7.1.1 General. A forfeiture order may be made in addition to another disposal of the case. Where a person is convicted of an offence and the court is satisfied that any property which was in his possession or under his control at the time of his apprehension had been used for the purpose of committing or facilitating the commission of any offence, or was intended by him to be used for that purpose, that property is liable to forfeiture. Any property so forfeited may be disposed of as the court may direct.[1] Facilitating the commission of an offence includes taking any steps after it had been committed for the purpose of disposing of any property to which it relates or of avoiding apprehension or detection.[2]

7.1.2 Any offence. The general power of forfeiture in the 1975 Act extends not only to the offence of which the person is convicted but also to property used or intended to be used in the commission of "any offence". In *Donnelly* v. *H.M. Advocate* the offender was convicted of possessing cannabis resin with intent to supply.[3] £1,047 which had been found hidden in his house was ordered to be forfeited. He appealed against the forfeiture order on the ground that none of the money could have related to an offence of an intention of future supply and it was not all proved to have any connection with the previous drug supply. The forfeiture order was upheld. It was considered competent under s. 223(1)(b) of the 1975 Act. The trial judge had been entitled to be satisfied that the money was intended to be used by the offender for the purpose of committing an offence and, for that matter, an offence under the Misuse of Drugs Act 1971.

7.1.3 Probation and absolute discharge. In summary proceedings, by virtue of ss. 383 and 384 of the 1975 Act, the court does not proceed to conviction when discharging a person absolutely or placing him on probation. As the general forfeiture power is dependant upon conviction, a forfeiture order cannot be made in summary proceedings in conjunction with an absolute discharge or a probation order.

Certain other statutory provisions specifically provide that forfeiture may accompany a probation order.[4] Where a convicted thief is found in possession of any tool or other object from which the commission of theft can be inferred, the court does have power to order forfeiture of the tool or other objects concerned and place the offender on probation or grant an absolute discharge.[5]

7.1.4 Powers exercisable on and irrespective of conviction. Some forfeiture powers can be exercised only on conviction while others are exercisable whether or not proceedings are brought. Thus, an offensive weapon may only be forfeited after a conviction,[6] whereas tools for making forgeries or false implements may in certain instances be seized irrespective of whether criminal proceedings are taken.[7]

7.1.5 Forfeiture of motor vehicle. A motor car has been forfeited where the offender pled guilty to stealing £400 worth of copper cable from a railway line with the aid of his car. The appeal court commented: "When the sheriff came to impose a penalty, he realised at once the crime could not have been committed without the use of a motor car." Lord Justice-General Emslie indicated that the court was entirely satisfied that the sheriff had been right to forfeit the car and the appeal was "resoundingly refused". The court took the view that any fine which would have met the circumstances of the case would have required the disposal of the car anyway to pay the fine and that the sheriff had saved the appellant the trouble of finding a market for the car at a price which would have come within striking distance of the amount of any fine.[8]

A van valued at £1,500 was forfeited after it had been used to load tiles worth £350 into it from a building site, in addition to fines of £200 being imposed on each of the two co-accused. The sentence was upheld by the Court of Criminal Appeal, observing that if criminals use vehicles for the purpose of committing or facilitating the commission of an offence, then they are liable to have those vehicles forfeited. If the offender was prepared to use a valuable vehicle then he did so at his own risk.[9] Similar sentiments were expressed in relation to the forfeiture of a car used in connection with thefts by shoplifting.[10]

An order to forfeit a motor vehicle being driven by an accused person while he was disqualified from so doing has been quashed by the Court of Criminal Appeal. It seemed to the court that the current terms of s. 436(1) of the 1975 Act did not apply to the offence of driving while disqualified. If the section had applied, the appeal court considered that the notice of penalties would have had to have contained a reference to forfeiture for forfeiture to have been competent.[11] The government's view would appear to have been that the general forfeiture provisions did permit forfeiture of vehicles in respect of all road traffic offences.[12]

This matter has now been clarified by s. 37 of the Road Traffic Act 1991. Where a person commits an offence under the Road Traffic Act 1988 punishable with imprisonment or an offence of culpable homicide by driving, attempting to drive or being in charge of a vehicle, failing to provide a specimen for analysis or failing to stop and give information or report an accident, the vehicle is to be regarded as being used for the purpose of committing the offence.[13] It may therefore be forfeited.

7.1.6 Innocent owners. One of the major deficiencies of the forfeiture sections is that no express account is taken of the innocent person with an interest in the property liable to forfeiture. If a car was used in the commission of a robbery it would be competent for the court to order its forfeiture. However, it might subsequently transpire that the car had been loaned to the convicted person or was owned by a hire-purchase company. It would therefore not be the convicted person who suffered but the innocent owner. While the owner may have a claim against that person, he may have no funds to meet it and the owner would generally prefer to have his property returned to him.

In order to overcome this problem the High Court of Justiciary has allowed bills of suspension to be brought by the owners, although it is unusual to have such bills introduced by a party other than the convicted person.[14]

As long ago as 1974 Lord Justice-General Emslie, commenting on the previous general provision contained in s. 23 of the Criminal Justice Act 1972, described it as a "remarkable omission" that Parliament had failed to provide any machinery to protect the rights of the true owners of forfeited property.[15] Section 23(3) did provide for delivery of forfeited property to its true owner but did not apply to Scotland. The current English provision contained in s. 43(3) of the Powers of Criminal Courts Act 1973 provides for a six-month period after the making of the order during which the innocent owner may apply to the court for the property to be returned to him.

A distinction has to be drawn where the owner of the property is not the offender but is nonetheless not entirely "innocent". Where a boat and nets belonging to the father of one of the offenders and the grandfather of the other was used in the commission of an offence, the sheriff was entitled to order forfeiture of the boat and nets as the owner had been aware that his son had wrongly obtained a fishing permit in his name and that the offenders had free access to the boat and nets.[16]

The Scottish Law Commission has proposed that an innocent party in Scotland should also be able to apply to the court which made the order for it to be reviewed and asks whether a six-month period should be imposed.[17] It recognises that this might present practical difficulties in the retention of forfeited property since the clerk of court would be unable to dispose of it if a review was still competent.

7.1.7 Specific statutory provisions. There is some dispute as to whether the general statutory provisions contained in the 1975 Act can be applied if a particular statutory provision is not applicable. *Donnelly* v. *H.M. Advocate*[18] indicated that they could, *Aitken* v. *Lockhart*[19] that they could not.

7.1.8 Warrant to search for forfeited articles. A search warrant may be issued in respect of an article where a court has made an order for its forfeiture. The warrant may be issued by the court, a sheriff, magistrate or any justice of the peace. The issuer of the warrant would first require to be satisfied on information on oath that there was reasonable cause to believe that the article was to be found in the place or premises and that admission thereto had been refused or that a refusal of admission was apprehended.[20]

7.1.9 Proposals for reform. The Scottish Law Commission has proposed that it should be made clear that courts have the power when ordering that property be forfeited that the proceeds of its sale should be directed towards payment of a compensation order to the victim.[21]

A further matter which the Commission raises is whether heritable and incorporeal property as well as moveable property could be forfeited. The forfeiture sections refer to "any property" which was in the possession or under the control of the accused at the time of his arrest. They are not expressly limited to moveable property. The situation is complicated by the English interpretation of the identical phrase as being confined to personal and excluding real property. In *R. v. Khan; R. v. Crawley* the Court of Appeal quashed an order for a house controlled by the accused and used in drug offences to be forfeited under s. 43(1) of the Powers of Criminal Courts Act 1973.[22] However, it did so on the basis that the subsection had to be read along with s. 43(4) which was limited to personal property but which does not apply to Scotland.

It is therefore by no means certain that the English reasoning would be applicable in Scotland, although the House of Lords in *R. v. Cuthbertson* also indicated that personal property was envisaged.[23] The Commission at this stage does not take a stand on the point but is content to canvass views.

In addition to the general forfeiture provisions, there are also the many specific forfeiture provisions in individual statutes. The Commission raises the possibility of consolidating them all into one single provision but envisages that this would be neither prudent nor practical.

The Commission considers whether forfeiture should continue to be restricted to those items in the possession or under the control of the convicted person at the time of his apprehension. It suggests that this should be replaced by a wider formula such as "property which was at the time of the offence or at the time of his apprehension in his ownership or possession or under his control".

Although at present a forfeiture order cannot be made in summary proceedings in conjunction with a probation order or an absolute discharge, the Commission recommends that a forfeiture order should be competent in these cases.

7.2 Confiscation

7.2.1 General.

Confiscation is increasingly being used as a sanction in numerous jurisdictions. The current Scottish legislation concerns confiscation of the proceeds of drug trafficking. While as yet these provisions have been seldom invoked, it can be only a matter of time before more of such cases arise and are reported. However, this legislation has not entirely met the pressures behind confiscation. The extension of confiscation orders to other cases is currently under review, the Scottish Law Commission having issued a discussion paper on the options for reform.[24]

The main purpose of confiscation is that it should attempt to strip an offender of any gains which he had derived from his criminal activity and to put him back into the position he was in before that activity had occurred.

Although the Scottish legislation relates only to drug trafficking, in England the scope of confiscation orders has already been extended. The Criminal Justice Act 1988 empowered courts in England and Wales to make orders for the confiscation of the proceeds of a much wider range of offences. However, before a court can make an order confiscating the proceeds of a non-drug related criminal offence, there is a restriction that it must first be satisfied that the offender has benefited from the offence of which he has been convicted or from that offence taken with some other offence of which he is convicted in the same proceedings.

This may be contrasted with the drug trafficking provisions which permit much of the property belonging to the offender to be confiscated unless it can be shown not to be derived from drug trafficking. There is a further restriction which is designed to exclude the more trivial cases, limiting confiscation orders under this Act to instances where the amount involved exceeds £10,000.

The Prevention of Terrorism (Temporary Provisions) Act 1989, which applies to the whole of the United Kingdom, allows courts, on conviction of an offence of soliciting or providing terrorist funds, to order the forfeiture of any money or other property in the possession or control of the convicted person at the time of the offence.

Further provisions on confiscation are to be found in the Criminal Justice (International Co-operation) Act 1990 which implements the United Nations Convention against Illicit Traffic in Narcotic Drugs and Psychotropic Substances signed in Vienna on 20 December 1988. This contains additional offences of concealing or transferring the proceeds of drug trafficking.

7.2.2 Development of confiscation powers. In the United Kingdom the case which was the most influential in bringing about change was that of *R. v. Cuthbertson*.[25] £750,000 of the profits from the manufacture and sale of lysergic acid (LSD) had been traced by the prosecution to assets which were still in the hands of those convicted. After orders had been made that these assets were to be forfeited, on appeal the House of Lords held that it had not been the intention of Parliament that s. 27(1) of the Misuse of Drugs Act 1971 (power to order forfeiture of "anything shown . . . to relate to the offence") should be used to strip drug traffickers of the profits of their enterprises. The power could only be used in relation to something tangible connected with the offence and not in relation to property situated abroad. Thereafter, a report containing recommendations for reform in England and Wales compiled by a committee chaired by Sir Derek Hodgson was published in 1984.[26]

Although involving only a small sum, an earlier Scottish example of a case where money was seized which might have been the proceeds of drug trafficking is *Caithness v. Bowman*.[27] The pursuer had been detained by the police when in possession of a bag containing £11,000. Suspecting that he had been trafficking in drugs, the police obtained a search warrant and found a further £300 in his house. He sought the return of the £300 from the chief constable, who refused to accede, relying on s. 83 of the Civic Government (Scotland) Act 1982. The sheriff granted decree, commenting that the money might well have been acquired in connection with, or be the profit from, drug trafficking but that s. 83 did not extend to property not physically in the possession of the pursuer at the time of his detention.

The Scottish Law Commission received a reference relating to confiscation from the Secretary of State for Scotland on 8 February 1985.[28] When legislation for England and Wales providing for confiscation of the proceeds of drug trafficking was introduced into Parliament soon after, becoming the Drug Trafficking Offences Act 1986, the reference was suspended enabling Scottish legislation broadly in line with the English provisions to be introduced in the Criminal Justice (Scotland) Act 1987.[29]

7.2.3 The drug trafficking powers. In Scotland where a person is convicted in the High Court of Justiciary, or is remitted there for sentence, for a drug trafficking offence, on the application of the prosecutor the court may make an order requiring the person to pay an amount not exceeding what it assesses to be the value of the proceeds of the person's drug trafficking or the value of the property which might be realised if that is less.[30] The order is regarded as a sentence and may therefore be appealed. An unusual feature of the court's power is that in assessing the proceeds of drug trafficking it may assume that any property held by the offender since his conviction or transferred to him at any time since a date six years before he was indicted was received by him as a payment or reward in connection with drug trafficking carried on by him.[31]

7.2.4 Procedural aspects. The prosecutor may lodge with the clerk of court a statement with any matters considered relevant to the assessment of the value of the offender's proceeds from drug trafficking. The court may then require the offender to indicate to what extent he accepts each allegation in the statement and, in so far as he does not accept any such allegation, to indicate the basis of his non-acceptance. Failure to comply may be treated as accepting the allegation.[32]

It is unclear what should happen in drug trafficking cases when a statement which has been lodged by a prosecutor is challenged by the offender. Section 4 of the 1987 Act does not expressly lay down any procedure. While there is no general practice of conducting hearings in Scotland to resolve disputes of fact prior to sentence, any significant dispute should be settled by hearing evidence.[33] The question of which rules should be adopted in any such hearing is further complicated by the power in s. 3(5) of the 1987 Act to remit difficult questions of law or of fact to the Court of Session for a decision. On deciding the question the Court of Session will then transmit the case back to the High Court. The steps to be taken when such a remit is made are set out in Rule of Court 201D.

Under the 1987 Act once a confiscation order has been made an administrator may be appointed to realise the offender's estate. After payment of expenses, the property or the proceeds realised are to be applied towards the satisfaction of the confiscation order.[34]

7.2.5 Enforcement. Provision is also made under the 1987 Act for restraint orders which freeze an offender's assets and for the enforcement of confiscation orders. Where a confiscation order is imposed but unpaid, the offender is liable to a further sentence of imprisonment in lieu of payment. That period does not commence until the expiry of any other period of imprisonment imposed on him in the proceedings.[35]. The Criminal Justice (International Co-operation) Act 1990 also imposes a liability for interest on sums unpaid under confiscation orders, with the amount of interest being treated as part of the amount to be recovered under the confiscation order. In Scotland a sheriff may, on the application of the prosecutor, increase the term of imprisonment fixed in respect of the confiscation order if the amount of interest would increase the period of imprisonment which was applicable.[36]

Notes

1. 1975 Act, ss. 223(1) and 436(1) as substituted by the 1980 Act, s. 83(2), Sch. 7 para. 71. See D. Kelly, "Forfeiture", 1991 *Scottish Law Gazette* 7.
2. 1975 Act, ss. 223(2) and 436(2).
3. 1984 S.C.C.R. 93.
4. *E.g.* Firearms Act 1968.
5. Civic Government (Scotland) Act 1982, s. 58.
6. Prevention of Crime Act 1953, s. 1.
7. Forgery and Counterfeiting Act 1981, s. 7. See also s. 24 and the Copyright, Designs and Patents Act 1988, ss. 108 and 195.
8. *Carruthers* v. *MacKinnon* 1986 S.C.C.R. 643.
9. *McQueeney* v. *Carmichael* 1991 S.C.C.R. 221.
10. *Wallace* v. *MacDougall* 1991 S.C.C.R. 962. See also *Reid* v. *Houston* 1992 S.C.C.R. 442.
11. *Findlay* v. *McNaughtan* 1991 S.C.C.R. 321.
12. *The Road User and the Law*, White Paper, 1989, para. 4.13.
13. 1975 Act, ss. 223(1A) and 436(1A), as inserted by the Road Traffic Act 1991, s. 37.

14. *Loch Lomond Sailings Limited* v. *Hawthorn* 1962 J.C. 8; 1962 S.L.T. 6; J. W. *Semple and Sons* v. *MacDonald* 1963 J.C. 90; 1963 S.L.T. 295.
15. *Lloyds and Scottish Finance Ltd.* v. *H.M. Advocate* 1974 J.C. 24, 27.
16. *Bain* v. *Wilson* 1987 S.C.C.R. 270.
17. *Forfeiture and Confiscation*, No. 82, June 1989.
18. 1984 S.C.C.R. 93.
19. 1989 S.C.C.R. 368.
20. 1975 Act, ss. 224 and 437.
21. *Forfeiture and Confiscation*, No. 82, June 1989.
22. [1982] 1 W.L.R. 1405; [1982] 3 All E.R. 969.
23. [1981] A.C. 470; [1980] 3 W.L.R. 89; [1980] 2 All E.R. 401.
24. *Forfeiture and Confiscation*, No. 82, June 1989. See D. Kelly, "Confiscation", 1991 S.L.T. 103.
25. [1981] A.C. 470; [1980] 3 W.L.R. 89; [1980] 2 All E.R. 401.
26. *The Profits of Crime and Their Recovery* (London, 1984).
27. 1987 S.C.L.R. 642.
28. *Twentieth Annual Report 1984–85*, para. 2.12.
29. Herein referred to as the "1987 Act".
30. 1987 Act, s. 1.
31. 1987 Act, s. 3.
32. 1987 Act, s. 4.
33. Renton and Brown's *Criminal Procedure* (5th edn.), para. 10–71.
34. 1987 Act, ss. 13–22.
35. 1987 Act, s. 7.
36. Criminal Justice (International Co-operation) Act 1990, s. 15.

CHAPTER 8

ROAD TRAFFIC DISPOSALS

8.1 Disqualification

8.1.1 General. Where a person is convicted of an offence involving obligatory disqualification, the court must order him to be disqualified for such period not less than 12 months as the court thinks fit unless the court for special reasons thinks fit to order him to be disqualified for a shorter period or not to order him to be disqualified.[1]

The purpose of disqualification is to afford protection to the public.[2] A judge should determine the period of disqualification appropriate to each charge and not on the basis of the driver's conduct as a whole.[3]

Where disqualification is discretionary, the Court of Criminal Appeal has no right to interfere with the exercise of the sheriff's discretion unless it is plainly demonstrated that the sheriff proceeded upon a misdirection or failed to take into account relevant and material circumstances. It will not normally interfere with the sheriff's decision on disqualification unless the sheriff has exercised his discretion wrongly by taking some factor into account which he should not have done or by failing to take some factor into account which he should have done.[4] One such factor which may be taken into account in determining whether disqualification would be appropriate, is premenstrual tension.[5]

If the case is to be adjourned or continued for a medical report, if sentence is deferred or if a convicted person is remitted to the High Court of Justiciary for sentence, an interim disqualification may be imposed.[6]

8.1.2 Personal appearance. In those circumstances where disqualification is a possible consequence of conviction, courts should adhere to the practice of giving the offender an opportunity to address them in mitigation.[7] Such situations would arise where the accused pled guilty by letter. In general, it is a sensible practice to defer sentence in order to give the offender the opportunity of appearing and addressing the court on the subject of why disqualification should not be imposed.[8] If not afforded such an opportunity, the appeal court may give weight to circumstances unknown to the sheriff and quash the disqualification.[9] Even if the circumstances were unchanged, the question of disqualification would be open for consideration by the appeal court and the disqualification might be quashed.[10]

8.1.3 Concurrent. Courts have no power to impose consecutive periods of disqualification. In the absence of any statutory provision empowering the courts to make a disqualification consecutive, it is incompetent for them to do so. Accordingly, any disqualification order, even one resulting from the totting up of penalty points, must be made concurrent with other disqualifications.[11]

8.1.4 Short periods of disqualification. As the purpose of disqualification is to afford protection to the public, it has been argued that a short period of disqualification might be regarded as irrational. If disqualification would result in the driver losing his employment, it has been considered of little sense to restrict the period of disqualification. The protection afforded to the public by such a disqualification would be very small and it would be paid for at the enormous price of loss of livelihood. Thus, a £100 fine and two months' disqualification have been quashed and a £400 fine and five penalty points substituted.[12]

Although a short period of disqualification might not have provided as much protection to the public as a longer period, it has always been regarded as competent to impose a short period of disqualification in a suitable case. Such a short period of disqualification was justified as a penalty which had both a punitive and a deterrent effect.[13]

However, short periods of disqualification are encouraged by the provisions of the Road Traffic Act 1991. Section 33, for example, dispenses with the need to apply for a fresh licence where the disqualification is for less than 56 days.[14] Greater use might therefore be made of this measure in future.

8.1.5 Standard practice. While a judge may wish to make it plain to members of the public that it is important that a particular statutory offence is not committed, it is not appropriate for him to adopt a standard practice of disqualifying in all such cases unless exceptional hardship would be involved. There would be a risk that the judge would disable himself from exercising his discretion in all cases which came before him.[15]

8.1.6 Disqualification in excess of minimum. A view that an offence of failure to provide a specimen for analysis must attract more than the minimum period of disqualification is totally erroneous. It may be held on the basis that not to provide one would place a person refusing to give a sample in a more favourable position than, for example, someone giving a sample which was twice the permitted limit. However, to impose a minimum of say two years in all cases for this reason would have the effect of ignoring the minimum period of disqualification of one year laid down by Parliament. The proper course is always to look at the offence in the light of all of the relevant circumstances.[16] However, in exercising his discretion, a judge would be entitled to disqualify in excess of the minimum period if the circumstances warranted it.[17]

8.1.7 Absolute discharge and probation. It is now competent to combine disqualification with either an absolute discharge or probation.[18]

8.1.8 Disqualification for life. In considering the imposition of an order disqualifying a driver for life, a court is entitled to take into account not only the gravity of the offence but also the condition and declared intentions of the driver. The appeal court has upheld the disqualification for life of a driver who pled guilty to driving while his ability to do so was impaired by drugs, contrary to the then current s. 5(1) of the Road Traffic Act 1972. He suffered from severe hearing impairments, depression, epilepsy and spasticity of the lower limbs and he had informed the sheriff that he had no intention of driving again. In these circumstances, the appeal court could not fault the sheriff's decision to disqualify him for life.[19]

Where it is appropriate to select a period of disqualification for life in the public interest, there is nothing wrong in explaining to the convicted person why that has been done. If the explanation is that it is in the public interest that he should not be on the road until his drinking habits have been controlled, it is neither unreasonable nor improper to point out that he may reapply for his licence at any time after five years.[20]

Disqualification for life for a second drink offence was not considered to be harsh and oppressive where a sheriff had obtained a medical report which had described the driver as having been an excessive drinker for the previous four years.[21] It was deemed to be in the public interest to disqualify him for life in the knowledge that he could reapply for a licence in five years' time.

8.1.9   Disqualification until driving test passed.

Prior to the Road Traffic Act 1991. The imposition of the requirement to pass a driving test has not been regarded as being punitive. A number of considerations were of relevance, one of which was that in general the longer the period of disqualification the more important it was that there should be a driving test before the driver again obtained a full licence.[22] The court should not simply order the offender "to resit a test" since that would not necessarily require the test to be passed, but should echo the statutory provision.[23]

The order to resit the test was not seen as a penalty but as designed to cater for the situation where a person, through disqualification, may have lost the skills which it was assumed were possessed at the time the disqualification was imposed. Accordingly, a judge could not impose a short period of disqualification and order the offender to resit a test solely in order to ensure that the offender passed a driving test.[24]

A single instance of a lapse of attention, even to a gross degree, which constituted careless driving would not necessarily bring into question the driver's competence to drive and call for the imposition of an order to resit a driving test. The advanced years of a driver guilty of an error of judgment constituting careless driving would not in themselves be sufficient to support the fact that he was not a competent driver.[25] Conversely, in a thoroughly bad case of careless driving where the driver had little driving experience, an order to resit the test was deemed appropriate in order to ensure that at the end of a three-year period of disqualification the driver had lost none of the skills, such as they were, which he had acquired while he had a licence.[26]

An order to resit the test was justifiable in the case of a 20-year-old who was disqualified for two years, who had not driven for longer than 18 months and whose reliability as a careful driver was very much in question, having been convicted of drink driving and careless driving.[27]

Where a person who already had ten penalty points on his licence was convicted of careless driving which was of such a nature that it indicated that he was lacking in the necessary qualities of discipline and responsibility, an order to resit the test after a six-month totting-up disqualification was justified. The sheriff was entitled to conclude that it was essential that the offender's competence to drive should be tested again.[28]

After the Road Traffic Act 1991. Under the revised statutory provisions brought into force on 1 July 1992, re-testing is obligatory in cases of serious offences such as on conviction of culpable homicide by the driver of a motor vehicle, causing death by dangerous driving or dangerous driving. Re-testing may also be ordered when a person is convicted of any other offence involving obligatory endorsement. The test will be the normal one of competency to drive unless the offence involved obligatory disqualification or the offender is disqualified under the totting-up provisions, in which case the test will be an extended driving test.[29]

8.1.10 Obligatory and discretionary disqualification in failure to provide specimen. A person who, without reasonable excuse, fails to provide a specimen when required to do so by a constable in the course of an investigation into a contravention of ss. 4 or 5 of the Road Traffic Act 1988 is guilty of an offence and is liable to disqualification.[30] The disqualification is obligatory where the specimen was required to ascertain ability to drive or the proportion of alcohol at the time the offender was driving or attempting to drive and otherwise discretionary.[31]

In a case in 1981 it was held that if it was not shown that the person refusing to supply the specimen was the driver, the disqualification would not be obligatory. Even although the appellant in one case was in the vehicle, as there was more than one occupant, in the absence of proof that he was driving, he might well have been merely a passenger.[32] In such circumstances, disqualification was discretionary.

In 1984 as a result of amendments originally made in the Transport Act 1981, the determining factor was held by the sheriff to be not whether or not a person was driving or attempting to drive but whether the police thought that he was driving or attempting to drive. If they were investigating a possible offence of driving or attempting to drive while unfit, failure to comply and provide a specimen would result in obligatory disqualification irrespective of whether or not the person had been driving or attempting to drive.[33] This meant that a person refusing to provide a specimen would be liable to obligatory disqualification even if he had no connection with the vehicle at all. An appeal was dismissed by the High Court of Justiciary without delivering opinions.

This case has since been distinguished on the basis that the charge to which the accused pled guilty included the words "and it will be shown that the said specimens of breath were required to ascertain your ability to drive or the proportion of alcohol in your breath at the time you were attempting to drive a motor vehicle". If the accused had not been attempting to drive a motor vehicle, he should not have pled guilty to the charge.

The Court of Criminal Appeal has indicated in 1986 that the statutory provision makes it quite plain that obligatory disqualification will only arise in cases where an accused was in fact driving or attempting to drive. The words "at the time offender was driving or attempting to drive" in the Schedule means just that.[34] Although this decision related to the provisions of the Road Traffic Act 1972 as amended, they are identical in this respect to those in the Road Traffic Offenders Act 1988 and so this interpretation will still be applicable.

8.1.11 Social enquiry report. Where the court orders a social enquiry report it should await receipt of that report before considering whether to disqualify the accused person for driving. The appeal court has quashed a disqualification order and an order to resit a driving test where the sheriff imposed them at one diet, called for a social enquiry report and imposed a fine at the resumed diet.[35] It was considered essential for justice that all of the possible elements in sentence should be considered at the same time. The background report turned out to be highly relevant to the question of sentence as a whole.

8.1.12 Special reasons.

Procedure. The procedure to be adopted in establishing special reasons has been set out in *McLeod* v. *Scoular*.[36] The onus is on the accused person to establish the special reasons for imposing less than the requisite 12 months period of disqualification. Accordingly, it is for the defence to place before the court evidence to justify the court in holding that special reasons have been established. The prosecution should in turn have the opportunity of placing before the court evidence which qualifies or contradicts the other evidence.

Four situations might arise. First, the prosecution might agree that the facts as stated by the defence are true. The court would then be entitled to proceed on the facts so stated but could adjourn for fuller particulars if that were thought necessary for the proper disposal of the plea.

Second, if the case has proceeded to trial and the facts founded upon have already been explored in evidence the court might decide the issue forthwith if it is not thought necessary to have any further enquiry.

Third, the prosecution might dispute any of the material facts relied on by the defence. Unless the court is of the opinion that these facts would not constitute special reasons, the proper course for the court to follow is to order a further hearing of the case to allow the defence to lead evidence in support of these facts. The prosecution would have the right to cross-examine on this evidence or to lead evidence in rebuttal of it.

Fourth, at the time of the trial the prosecution may not be in a position to admit, deny or qualify the facts submitted by the defence. In that case, the proper course is for the court to follow the same procedure as in the third situation.

Driving. Special reasons for not imposing a mandatory period of disqualification for driving involve some act of emergency which leads the motorist to drive in spite of his condition or ban, because there is no other way of achieving some wholly necessary object. Where a person, apprehensive that a lorry might be stolen, drove it 50 yards into his employer's yard while his blood alcohol content exceeded the limit, it was held that other means of protecting the lorry were not first explored and the explanation did not constitute a special reason. [37]

After a disabled driver was involved in a road accident in which no one was hurt while driving a mini-car owned by the Scottish Home and Health Department, as a condition of having the car he was required to report any damage to it to the police. He proceeded to his son-in-law's house where he had a drink before driving to report the accident to the police. Since there was no emergency requiring him to drive the car at all at the time – he could have telephoned or written to the police station – there were no special reasons for not disqualifying.[38]

There were special reasons for not disqualifying when, after an accident where a car had become embedded in a snow drift in such a way as to block the road for other vehicles, a passenger with an excess of alcohol took over from the driver.[39] Special reasons were also established where a person had left his car on a main road after it had broken down. On returning later he had pushed the car and steered it into a parking space where it had collided with a parked car. Moving the car from the main road in the interests of safety was deemed to constitute a special reason.[40] The disqualification was reduced from three years to one year.

A medical emergency could constitute a special reason. A medical emergency in this regard would be an unexpected situation in which a person who had been drinking but not intending to drive was impelled to drive a car by a sudden medical necessity. Thus, in one case a person was awakened after retiring to bed following a party by a guest who was pregnant, had started to bleed heavily and feared a miscarriage. When he drove her to the hospital while he still had an excess of alcohol, there were special reasons for not disqualifying.[41]

The fact that a person was driving in order to escape from assailants, where the driver had not intended to drive and did so only because of an unforeseen situation which arose, may constitute a special reason for not disqualifying.[42]

In England, the fact that a person only drove for a very short distance is capable of amounting to a special reason for not disqualifying. It would depend on the particular case whether the circumstances did amount to a special reason.[43] The Court of Criminal Appeal has been referred to this English rule but has given it little cognisance. Where a car was driven a short distance in a car park, it was considered to have been all too likely that the vehicle would come into contact with other road users, which was in fact what did happen. There was therefore no special reason for not disqualifying.[44]

Failure to provide specimen for analysis. Different considerations apply in assessing a special reason for refusing to supply a specimen for analysis from assessing a special reason for driving. Where it is a specimen that is refused, it is not appropriate to consider whether there was an emergency which justified driving with an excess of alcohol. Those authorities recognising certain types of emergencies as special reasons for driving would not necessarily be relevant. The special reasons must relate to the refusal to provide a specimen and not to the driving of the vehicle.

Thus, it was not a special reason to refuse to provide a specimen because the driver was on his way to join a mountain rescue team with a view to assisting in the saving of life.[45] This followed an English case where it was not a special reason to refuse because the driver had a cut hand and was on his way to hospital.[46] Nor was it a special reason that the accused had driven only for a brief moment in order to reposition the parking of a car.[47]

In determining whether or not special reasons exist it is always important to have regard to matters of public safety and one issue must be whether the safety of the public would be prejudiced by refraining from disqualification. While it is not a special reason in a case of failing to provide a sample for analysis for someone to have been drinking but only to an extent below the permitted level, nor would it be a special reason that the accused had not in fact been drinking, if the accused was teetotal, that is, a total abstainer, that may be a special case. With a total abstainer there would be no reason to apprehend danger to the public from the person driving after having consumed alcohol and so a judge might competently hold that special reasons were made out.[48] However, that would be an unusual and special circumstance.[49]

Premenstrual tension has not been seen as constituting a special reason and the court has observed that it found difficulty in conceiving what could be a special reason for refusing to provide a specimen.[50]

As, except in very special circumstances, it does not matter whether or not alcohol has been consumed by the accused in a case of failing to provide a specimen, there would be no reason to hold a proof in mitigation to establish whether alcohol had been consumed in order to see if special reasons existed for not disqualifying.[51]

8.1.13 Disqualification where vehicle used to commit offence. The courts in Scotland have been given the power previously possessed by courts in England and Wales to disqualify an offender who used a vehicle to commit or facilitate an offence. This includes taking steps after its commission to dispose of property or to avoid apprehension or detection. The power may be exercised in relation to all offences other than those triable only summarily.[52]

8.1.14 Courses for drink-drive offenders. As an experiment, provision has been made for the reduction of a period of disqualification of not less than 12 months where the offender satisfactorily completes an approved course of re-training. The reduction would be not less than three months and not more than a quarter of the unreduced period.[53]

8.2 Endorsement

8.2.1 General. Where a person is convicted of an offence involving obligatory endorsement, the court must order particulars of the conviction to be endorsed on his licence as well as particulars of any disqualification, or of the offence and any penalty points imposed.[54] However, if the court does not order the convicted person to be disqualified, it need not make an endorsement order if for special reasons it thinks fit not to do so.[55]

8.2.2 Previous endorsements. The Court of Criminal Appeal has on occasion gone beyond the bare terms of previous convictions as shown on a licence to consider the circumstances of the offences themselves. In a case where a lorry driver convicted of a speeding offence was liable to a mandatory period of disqualification by reason of the totting up of his previous endorsements, mitigating circumstances for reducing the length of the period were put forward and the appeal court continued the case to discover more about his previous convictions. Both turned out to be speeding offences involving the driving of a lorry on the "notorious A74" and the appeal against disqualification was dismissed.[56]

8.2.3 Special reasons for not endorsing.

As with special reasons for not disqualifying, it is for the offender to plead and establish special reasons for not endorsing.[57] As Lord Justice-General Emslie put it: "The drill in cases of this kind . . . is perfectly well settled . . ."[58] The reason for requiring the offender to raise the issue is to enable the Crown to consider the proposal that there may be special reasons inherent in the circumstances of the offence. It is not for the sheriff *ex proprio motu* to exercise a power not to endorse when the Crown has not had an opportunity of making representations upon that question. In particular, a sheriff ought never to exercise the power unless the issue has been raised specifically by the defence in the course of a trial or plea in mitigation.[59]

Factors which might constitute special reasons for not disqualifying may not carry the same or similar weight in relation to endorsement. While there may be no good or sufficient reason for taking a driver off the road, endorsement has no such immediate or public consequences. The factors which constitute special reasons for abstaining from endorsement may differ considerably from those which will be apposite in relation to disqualification.[60]

It would be hard to envisage circumstances surrounding the original police suspicion which could amount to a mitigation or extenuation of a refusal to provide a specimen for analysis or as being directly connected with the refusal.[61]

A distinction is to be drawn where an accused person pleads guilty by letter and brings to the notice of the court circumstances capable of constituting special reasons. The established principle and practice, which apply where there has been appearance by or on behalf of the accused person at the stage of sentence and which are particularly appropriate in cases where the accused is legally represented, require some adjustment when a plea of guilty is intimated by letter.[62]

It would be unjust to require that the accused should make express reference to "special reasons" in his letter and in addition specifically submit that his licence should not be endorsed. If the letter contains an account of circumstances which could competently constitute special reasons and the contents of the letter have come to the notice of the Crown (which would normally be so in tendering it to the court), the procedural requirements would be sufficiently complied with.[63] The court would accordingly be entitled to refrain from ordering endorsement.

8.2.4 Refraining from endorsement in construction and use cases. A person convicted of a contravention of the construction and use regulations relating to breach of a requirement as to brakes, steering-gear or tyres may prove that he did not know and had no reasonable cause to suspect that the facts of the case were such that the offence would be committed.

In respect of an offence of using a vehicle in a dangerous condition, a person may prove that he did not know and had no reasonable cause to suspect that the use of the vehicle involved a danger of injury to any person. If so, the court must not order him to be disqualified nor order his licence to be endorsed.[64]

Where a driver had deep cuts in the tyres of his lorry, the question was not what had caused the cuts but whether the driver had proved that he had no reasonable cause to suspect their presence.[65] As in such a case the onus is on the driver, it is up to him to lead evidence as to why he had no reasonable cause to suspect that the offence had been committed. If he fails to prove this, the penalty points will be endorsed on his licence.[66]

8.3 Notice of penalty

If a notice of penalty has not been served on the accused person in a summary case involving statutory offences the court cannot proceed to impose any penalty.[67] It may not therefore impose a fine or disqualification.

In such circumstances, on the occasions when an offence carries no penalty points, a court may order endorsement of a driving licence since that is not a penalty but merely a record of the conviction.[68] However, in the more normal case where an offence does carry with it penalty points, it is incompetent to order endorsement in the absence of a reference to the penalty points in the notice of penalties. It would be incompetent to order endorsement of the licence without also awarding the penalty points, and the penalty points could not be awarded in the absence of any reference to them in the notice of penalties.[69]

8.4   Previous convictions

The court may take into account any endorsement on a person's licence who has been convicted of an offence involving obligatory endorsement where the licence is produced to the court.[70]

If a driver has never held a driving licence, a printout from the licensing centre could not be placed before the court in place of it.[71] However, there is nothing wrong, where a driver is convicted and is unable to produce his licence, for the court to be invited to look at a printout, without the consent of the driver. It is the driver's obligation to produce his licence and if he cannot do so he has no good reason for denying the court the opportunity of finding out the relevant information from the printout which will often be available from the Crown.[72] A judge should not rely solely on his own recollection of previous convictions.[73]

In sentencing an offender for a road traffic contravention, such as a failure to provide a specimen for analysis, a judge is entitled to look at the offender's criminal history and to take from it that he shows little regard for law observance and that the road traffic offence was simply an illustration of the behaviour of someone who cared nothing for observance of the law in general. If it would be competent to impose imprisonment even for a first offence and there were previous non-road traffic convictions, the offender might properly be imprisoned for the road traffic offence.[74]

8.5   Penalty points

Where a person is convicted of an offence involving obligatory or discretionary disqualification, the number of penalty points to be attributed to the offence is set out in Sch. 2 of the Road Traffic Offenders Act 1988. In the case of an offence committed by aiding and abetting an offence involving obligatory disqualification, the number of penalty points is ten.[75] In general, if convicted of two or more such offences, the number of penalty points to be attributed to those which occurred on the same occasion is the highest number that would be attributed on conviction of one of them. However, the court has a discretion also to impose points for the other offences.[76]

For totting up purposes, the penalty points to be taken into account are any that are to be attributed to the offences of which the person is convicted and any that were on a previous occasion ordered to be endorsed on any licence held by him unless he has since that occasion and before the conviction been disqualified for driving under the totting-up procedure.[77] If any of the offences was committed more than three years before another, the penalty points in respect of that offence are not added to those in respect of the other.[78] This excludes points awarded in respect of any offence committed more than three years before the offence currently being dealt with by the court.[79]

8.6   Totting up

8.6.1   General. Where a person is convicted of an offence which involves obligatory or discretionary disqualification and the number of penalty points to be taken into account totals 12 or more, he must be disqualified for at least the minimum period unless the court is satisfied that there are grounds for mitigating the normal consequences of the conviction and limits or dispenses with the disqualification.[80]

The minimum period is six months if there has been no previous disqualification to be taken into account, one year if one, and two years if more than one disqualification is to be taken into account.[81] No account is to be taken of any circumstances that are alleged to make an offence not a serious one; nor should account be taken of hardship other than exceptional hardship or any circumstances in the preceding three years which have already been taken into account in limiting or dispensing with a disqualification.[82]

It is improper to mark the gravity of a particular offence by imposing a totting-up disqualification. This will mainly arise where it is argued that there is exceptional hardship. The gravity of the offence should be marked by an appropriate penalty and the disqualification should be considered separately.[83]

If an accused person is to suggest that exceptional hardship would result from loss of his licence, it is up to him to put proper material before the court so that the court can be satisfied or otherwise as to the validity of his submissions.[84]

The mitigating grounds include circumstances relating to the offender as well as to the offence. Thus, although an offender was driving without insurance, the fact that he genuinely believed that he was insured would be a ground of mitigation entitling the court to refrain from disqualifying.[85]

8.6.2 Exceptional hardship.

General. It is important that a court should examine very carefully any suggestion that exceptional hardship has been established and should only hold such established on the clearest possible evidence. Otherwise, the effect of the legislation dealing with penalty points and the totting-up procedure would become ineffective.[86] It is not necessary in the course of presenting grounds for mitigating the disqualification specifically to use the words "exceptional hardship".[87] If a request for a proof in mitigation is made by the defence on the question of exceptional hardship and is concurred in by the Crown, it is incumbent on the court to allow it to take place.[88]

There have been many cases turning upon the issue of exceptional hardship. Each case must depend upon its own circumstances. Recent cases may be grouped in terms of where loss of a licence would lead to loss of employment, loss of a house or something more than that.

Loss of employment. Loss of employment by itself is not sufficient to constitute exceptional hardship.[89] It is a commonplace consequence of disqualification for people whose livelihood depends upon holding a driving licence.

A submission that a driver would lose employment which he had just obtained if he were disqualified was described by the appeal court in an earlier case as being eloquent of an exceptional hardship if disqualification was imposed. In that case his wife who was pregnant with her first child had been admitted to hospital as an emergency on the day of his speeding offence.[90]

The Court of Criminal Appeal held in *Allan* v. *Barclay* that in order to establish exceptional hardship it would be necessary to demonstrate not only that the particular offender may lose his employment but that associated with that loss of employment were certain other circumstances which might involve reflected hardship of a serious kind upon the offender's business, family or long-term future prospects.[91]

Since then, the Court of Criminal Appeal has indicated that while this is the proper test, the court is now taking a much stricter view of this type of case. If the offender had nine penalty points on his licence and was going to take the risk of committing a further road traffic offence, then the consequences must have been clear to him. Even although it was suggested that 150 employees' jobs might be in jeopardy, the magistrate had properly exercised his discretion in deciding that there would be no exceptional hardship.[92]

Loss of employment and house. In one case loss of employment coupled with loss of a house through the consequent inability to pay a mortgage were held to involve exceptional hardship where it was not clear that the justice had realised that the appellant would lose his job.[93] However, an appeal court comprising the same judges on the very next day refused to interfere with the justice's decision. The justice had held that exceptional hardship was not established and disqualified a driver where disqualification would lead to loss of his job and loss of his house consequent upon his inability to pay his mortgage.[94]

The Court of Criminal Appeal has observed that because of previous decisions in that court an impression might have formed that there must inevitably be exceptional hardship if an appellant would be unable to pay a mortgage in the event of losing his employment through disqualification. This is not true in every case and it cannot be assumed that, just because the offender enjoys the benefit of a mortgage, that will mean that he will necessarily suffer exceptional hardship in the event of disqualification leading to loss of employment. There is no absolute rule about this and each case will depend on its own circumstances.[95]

A disqualification was withheld where it would have caused the driver to lose his employment and force him to sell his house, with consequent exceptional hardship not only for himself but also for his wife and children.[96] However, this was later described as a very special case and it is not authority for the proposition that in every case where an accused represents that he will lose his employment and be unable to pay the mortgage on his house, with unfortunate consequences for himself and his dependants, that will necessarily amount to exceptional hardship.[97]

While there have been instances where having to seek alternative employment and a new house were treated as exceptional hardship,[98] in general it may now be said that it is not enough to establish exceptional hardship merely to say that the offender will lose his employment or will be unable to maintain his mortgage commitments. Before there can be exceptional hardship the matter must go further than that.[99]

General practice. The appeal court has quashed a disqualification which would have put an end to a one-man business as a haulage contractor and would have had draconian effects on the driver and his family. The court also looked at the nature of the offence – driving with an unsafe load – which was not one of the most serious offences under the Road Traffic Act. These factors did amount to mitigating circumstances because of their exceptional hardship.[100]

There was exceptional hardship where disqualification would put in jeopardy the appellant's family home and a loan for their furniture, when he was trying to get back on his feet again after the loss of a job through no fault of his own.[101] However, where a sheriff took into account all such matters as the disqualification jeopardising a managing director's employment and that of other persons employed by the company, also causing hardship to his family, and decided that any hardship caused would not be exceptional, the appeal court upheld his decision.[102]

Disqualification would have caused exceptional hardship to a businessman who could not obtain the services of a hired driver due to the hours that he worked and whose business would have folded had he lost his licence, leading to the dismissal of six employees.[103]

A disqualification which would have involved loss of the driver's job, with the consequent inability to pay his mortgage, leading to the loss of his house, the inability to repay a loan to his employer and the probable break-up of his marriage would have caused exceptional hardship.[104]

When the loss of a driving licence would have resulted in the end of the driver's business, which employed three people, and the likely loss of his family home, there was exceptional hardship.[105]

The loss of a licence probably resulting in the loss of the offender's business, affecting his health and that of his wife and interfering with his child's education was deemed to be exceptional hardship.[106] Again, where an offender argued that in the event of disqualification his business would collapse, leading to loss of employment for himself and six other persons and adverse effects on his customers, exceptional hardship was established.[107]

Exceptional hardship was also established where a self-employed consulting engineer responsible for finding work for three self-employed contractors argued that if he lost his licence he would not be able to obtain contracts and the contractors would lose their employment; a six months' disqualification was reduced to one of three months.[108]

On the other hand, in a further case it was not sufficient that in the event of disqualification the offender's businesses would be adversely affected. The Court of Criminal Appeal reiterated that drivers were in danger of losing their licences under the totting-up procedure when they were nearing the limit of 12 points and that they should then be very careful indeed. In disregarding the dangers they may become the authors of their own misfortunes.[109]

8.7 Fixed penalties

As well as those cases dealt with before the courts, certain specified offences are taken out of the court system where the offender complies with an established procedure. A fixed penalty is then imposed.[110]

Notes

1. Road Traffic Offenders Act 1988, s. 34(1).
2. *Saunders* v. *MacGillivray* 1985 S.C.C.R. 385.
3. *McMurrich* v. *Cardle* 1988 S.C.C.R. 20.
4. *Tariq* v. *Carmichael* 1982 S.C.C.R. 488; *Henderson* v. *McNaughton* 1992 S.C.C.R. 767.
5. *Thomas* v. *Lowe* 1991 S.C.C.R. 943.
6. Road Traffic Offenders Act 1988, s. 26(3), as substituted by the Road Traffic Act 1991, s. 25.

7. *Stephens* v. *Gibb* 1984 S.C.C.R. 195; *Pickard* v. *Ingram* (1976) S.C.C.R. Supp. 142.
8. *McDonald* v. *MacGillivray* 1986 S.C.C.R. 28.
9. *Donaldson* v. *Aitchison* 1985 S.C.C.R. 43.
10. *Buchan* v. *Ingram* 1987 S.C.C.R. 509.
11. *Middleton* v. *Tudhope* 1986 J.C. 101; 1986 S.C.C.R. 241.
12. *Saunders* v. *MacGillivray* 1985 S.C.C.R. 385.
13. *Leslie* v. *McNaughton* 1991 S.C.C.R. 32.
14. Road Traffic Offenders Act 1988, s.37(1A), as inserted by the Road Traffic Act 1991, s.33.
15. *MacDonald* v. *MacGillivray* 1986 S.C.C.R. 28.
16. *Hynd* v. *Guild* 1986 S.C.C.R. 406.
17. *Reynolds* v. *Tudhope* 1987 S.C.C.R. 340; *Jamsheed* v. *Walkingshaw* 1989 S.C.C.R. 75.
18. Road Traffic Offenders Act 1988, s.46(3).
19. *Awadia* v. *Keane* 1983 S.C.C.R. 20.
20. *Beattie* v. *Ingram* 1986 S.C.C.R. 38.
21. *Wiseman* v. *Hillary* 1981 S.C.C.R. 103. See also *Smith* v. *Wilson* 1989 S.C.C.R. 395.
22. *Sweeney* v. *Cardle* 1982 S.C.C.R. 10; 1982 S.L.T. 312, following *R.* v. *Guilfoyle* [1973] 2 All E.R. 844; [1973] R.T.R. 272.
23. *Fraser* v. *Lockhart* 1992 S.C.C.R. 275.
24. *McLean* v. *Annan* 1986 S.C.C.R. 52. See also *Fraser* v. *Lockhart* 1992 S.C.C.R. 275.
25. *Tariq* v. *Carmichael* 1982 S.C.C.R. 488; *Harper* v. *Lockhart* 1992 S.C.C.R. 429.
26. *Holmes* v. *Stewart* 1983 S.C.C.R. 446.
27. *Harvie* v. *Cardle* 1986 S.C.C.R. 41.
28. *Neill* v. *Annan* 1990 S.C.C.R. 454.
29. Road Traffic Offenders Act 1988, s.36, as substituted by the Road Traffic Act 1991, s.32.
30. Road Traffic Act 1988, s.7(6).
31. Road Traffic Offenders Act 1988, s.34(1) and Sch. 2.
32. *Stewart* v. *Aitchison* 1981 S.C.C.R. 107, concerning s.9(3) of the Road Traffic Act 1972; *R.* v. *Page* [1981] R.T.R. 132 followed.
33. *McLellan* v. *Tudhope* 1984 S.C.C.R. 397, concerning the Road Traffic Act 1972, s.8(7) and Sch.4, part I, as substituted by the Transport Act 1981, Sch.9, para.21.
34. *Aird* v. *Valentine* 1986 S.C.C.R. 353, approving the dicta of Lord Justice-General Emslie in *Cardle* v. *Campbell* 1985 S.C.C.R. 309.
35. *Gallagher* v. *Cruickshank* (1973) S.C.C.R. Supp. 36.
36. 1974 J.C. 28; 1974 S.L.T. (Notes) 44. *Cf. Normand* v. *Cameron* 1992 S.C.C.R. 390 where this procedure was not followed by the sheriff.
37. *Skeen* v. *Irvine* (1980) S.C.C.R. Supp. 259.
38. *Copeland* v. *Pollock* (1976) S.C.C.R. Supp. 111, applying *Irvine* v. *Pollock* 1952 J.C. 51; 1952 S.L.T. 195. See also *Normand* v. *Cameron* 1992 S.C.C.R. 390.
39. *Riddell* v. *MacNeill* 1983 S.C.C.R. 26.
40. *Orttewell* v. *Allan* 1984 S.C.C.R. 208.
41. *Watson* v. *Hamilton* 1988 S.C.C.R. 13; 1988 S.L.T. 316, adopting *Brown* v. *Dyerson* [1969] 1 Q.B. 45.
42. *MacLeod* v. *MacDougall* 1988 S.C.C.R. 519; 1989 S.L.T. 151.
43. *Redmond* v. *Parry* [1986] R.T.R. 146.
44. *Mackay* v. *MacPhail* 1989 S.C.C.R. 622. See, however, *Lowe* v. *Mulligan* 1991 S.C.C.R. 551.

45. *Smith* v. *Nixon* 1984 S.C.C.R. 373; 1985 S.L.T. 192.
46. *Anderton* v. *Anderton* [1977] R.T.R. 424.
47. *Lamb* v. *Heywood* 1988 S.C.C.R. 42; 1988 S.L.T. 728.
48. *Tudhope* v. *O'Kane* 1986 S.C.C.R. 538.
49. *McDade* v. *Jessop* 1990 S.C.C.R. 156; 1990 S.L.T. 800.
50. *Scott* v. *Hamilton* 1988 S.C.C.R. 262.
51. *Emms* v. *Lockhart* 1987 S.C.C.R. 622; 1988 S.L.T. 222.
52. 1975 Act, ss. 223A and 436A, as inserted by the Road Traffic Act 1991, s. 39.
53. Road Traffic Offenders Act 1988, s. 34A, as inserted by the Road Traffic Act 1991, s. 30.
54. Road Traffic Offenders Act 1988, s. 44(1).
55. Road Traffic Offenders Act 1988, s. 44(2).
56. *Rozanski* v. *Ingram* 1981 S.C.C.R. 100. Compare *Connell* v. *Mitchell* 1909 S.C.(J.) 13; (1908) 5 Adam 641; 16 S.L.T. 669 and *Baker* v. *McFadyean* 1952 S.L.T. (Notes) 70.
57. *Tudhope* v. *Birbeck* 1979 S.L.T. (Notes) 47; *McNab* v. *Feeney* 1980 S.L.T. (Notes) 52.
58. *McNab* v. *Feeney* 1980 S.L.T. (Notes) 52, 53.
59. *Ibid.* The same applies to the power not to disqualify.
60. *McDade* v. *Jessop* 1990 S.C.C.R. 156; 1990 S.L.T. 800.
61. *Ibid.*
62. *Keane* v. *Perrie* 1982 S.C.C.R. 377; 1983 S.L.T. 63.
63. *Ibid.*
64. Road Traffic Offenders Act 1988, s. 48 as substituted by Road Traffic Act 1991, s. 48 and Sch. 4, para. 101.
65. *Forrest* v. *Annan* 1990 S.C.C.R. 619; 1992 S.L.T. 510.
66. *Ibid.*
67. 1975 Act, s. 311(5).
68. *Scott* v. *Annan* 1981 S.C.C.R. 172; 1982 S.L.T. 90.
69. *Tudhope* v. *Eadie* 1984 J.C. 6; 1983 S.C.C.R. 464; 1984 S.L.T. 178, which considered *Scott* v. *Annan* above and *Donnelly* v. *Shotton* 1983 S.C.C.R. 236; 1983 S.L.T. 657. This case was followed in *Miller* v. *Allan; England* v. *Allan* 1984 S.C.C.R. 28; 1984 S.L.T. 280.
70. Road Traffic Offenders Act 1988, s. 31.
71. *Anderson* v. *Allan* 1985 J.C. 88; 1985 S.C.C.R. 262.
72. *McCallum* v. *Scott* 1986 S.C.C.R. 645; 1987 S.L.T. 491.
73. *Brown* v. *Guild* 1988 S.C.C.R. 6.
74. *Goldie* v. *Tudhope* 1986 S.C.C.R. 414.
75. Road Traffic Offenders Act 1988, s. 28(1) and (2), as substituted by the Road Traffic Act 1991, s. 27.
76. Road Traffic Offenders Act 1988, s. 28(4) and (5).
77. Road Traffic Offenders Act 1988, s. 29(1); *Drummond* v. *MacKinnon* 1983 S.C.C.R. 289; 1983 S.L.T. 681.
78. Road Traffic Offenders Act 1988, s. 29(2). On the method of computation of time, see *Keenan* v. *Carmichael* 1991 S.C.C.R. 680; 1992 S.L.T. 814.
79. *MacNeill* v. *Low; MacNeill* v. *Wright* 1983 S.C.C.R. 6 (Sh. Ct.).
80. Road Traffic Offenders Act 1988, s. 35(1).
81. Road Traffic Offenders Act 1988, s. 35(2).
82. Road Traffic Offenders Act 1988, s. 35(4).
83. *Briggs* v. *Guild* 1987 S.C.C.R. 141; *Gray* v. *Jessop* 1988 S.C.C.R. 71.
84. *McFadyen* v. *Tudhope* 1986 S.C.C.R. 712.
85. *Carmichael* v. *Shevlin* 1992 S.C.C.R. 247; 1992 S.L.T. 1113.

86. *Holden* v. *MacPhail* 1986 S.C.C.R. 486. See also *Scott* v. *Scott* 1983 S.C.C.R. 458.
87. *Pender* v. *Keane* 1984 S.C.C.R. 325.
88. *Kyle* v. *McNaughton* 1990 S.C.C.R. 450.
89. *Richardson* v. *MacPhail* 1988 S.C.C.R. 27; *Mowbray* v. *Guild* 1989 S.C.C.R. 535.
90. *Pender* v. *Keane* 1984 S.C.C.R. 325.
91. 1986 S.C.C.R. 111.
92. *Coldwell* v. *Jessop* 1990 S.C.C.R. 224.
93. *Railton* v. *Houston* 1986 S.C.C.R. 428.
94. *Miller* v. *Ingram* 1986 S.C.C.R. 437.
95. *Ibid.* See also *Holden* v. *MacPhail* 1986 S.C.C.R. 486; *Richardson* v. *MacPhail* 1988 S.C.C.R. 27.
96. *Stephens* v. *Gibb* 1984 S.C.C.R. 195.
97. *Holden* v. *MacPhail* 1986 S.C.C.R. 486.
98. See *Briggs* v. *Guild* 1987 S.C.C.R. 141.
99. *Mowbray* v. *Guild* 1989 S.C.C.R. 535.
100. *North* v. *Tudhope* 1985 S.C.C.R. 161.
101. *Allan* v. *Barclay* 1986 S.C.C.R. 111. See the later case of *Miller* v. *Ingram* 1986 S.C.C.R. 437.
102. *Bibby* v. *MacDougall* 1990 S.C.C.R. 121.
103. *Robinson* v. *Aitchison* 1986 S.C.C.R. 511.
104. *Gray* v. *Jessop* 1988 S.C.C.R. 71.
105. *McFadyen* v. *Tudhope* 1986 S.C.C.R. 712.
106. *Mowbray* v. *Guild* 1989 S.C.C.R. 535.
107. *Marshall* v. *MacDougall* 1991 S.C.C.R. 231.
108. *McLaughlin* v. *Docherty* 1991 S.C.C.R. 227.
109. *Clumpas* v. *Ingram* 1991 S.C.C.R. 223.
110. See the Road Traffic Offenders Act 1988, Part III.

PART TWO

CHAPTER 9

SPECIFIC OFFENCES

9.1 Introduction

The Court of Criminal Appeal has not sought in the course of appeals to express views on how similar cases should be dealt with in the future. Each case must be dealt with according to its own circumstances. A judge must exercise his discretion in choosing an appropriate disposal and that discretion ought not to be fettered in any way. Assuming there is no procedural irregularity, the appeal court will only interfere if there has been a miscarriage of justice through the sentence being inappropriate or excessive.

However, an examination of previous cases in which the Court of Criminal Appeal has had to decide whether a judge has exercised his discretion correctly may be useful in ascertaining the proper exercise of a judge's discretion in future cases. An awareness of sentencing practice in other courts, including in the appeal court, may also assist in achieving consistency in sentencing.

9.2 Animals

9.2.1 Birds' eggs.

Kausen v. *Walkingshaw*
1990 S.C.C.R. 553
(Lords Wylie, Weir and Brand)

Two Germans earning £125 per week pled guilty to being in possession of nine peregrine falcon eggs. The maximum penalty was £2,000 per egg. They were each fined £6,000.

Sentence: for such an abominable offence Parliament had advisedly conferred on courts of summary jurisdiction power to impose heavy monetary penalties; the only real protection for these rare birds was knowledge on the part of those who set out to commit these offences that very heavy penalties would be incurred if they were caught; however, the sheriff had wrongly taken commercial considerations into account when they had not been part of the offences charged and the fines were quashed and fines of £5,000 imposed on each.

9.2.2 Cruelty to animals.

Braid v. *Brown*
1990 S.C.C.R. 33; 1990 S.L.T. 793
(Lord Justice-General Hope, Lords Brand and Cowie)

A dog groomer stitched up a cut on a dog without an effective anaesthetic. She was fined £100 and a compensation order of £144.50 was made in favour of the owner.

Sentence: upheld.

9.2.3 Dangerous dogs.

Normand v. *Freeman*
1992 S.C.C.R. 417; 1992 S.L.T. 598
(Lord Justice-Clerk Ross, Lords McCluskey and Kirkwood)

The respondent was convicted of having a pit bull terrier in a public place without it being muzzled, contrary to the Dangerous Dogs Act 1991, s. 1. The sheriff deferred sentence and did not order destruction of the dog. The prosecutor appealed by bill of advocation.

Sentence: bill passed and case remitted to the sheriff to order destruction of the dog in terms of s. 4(1) of the Act.

9.3 Assault

9.3.1 Assault and offensive weapon.

An offender may be sentenced separately for charges of assault and possession of an offensive weapon.[1]

9.3.2 Assault by driving car at someone.

McMillan v. *H.M. Advocate*
1987 S.C.C.R. 490; 1988 S.L.T. 211
(Lord Justice-Clerk Ross, Lords Robertson and McDonald)

The appellant was convicted of assault by driving a car at a police constable causing her to jump clear and fall to the pavement to her slight injury. He was sentenced to 18 months' imprisonment.

Sentence: the offence was a very serious one for which a custodial sentence was necessary but the sentence was quashed and one of six months' imprisonment imposed.

9.3.3 Assault by headbutting.

Glen v. McLeod

1982 S.C.C.R. 449

(Lord Justice-General Emslie, Lords Cameron and Avonside)

The appellant pled guilty to assaulting his uncle by butting him on the face and trying to kick and punch him. The victim had eight stitches inserted in his jaw. The appellant, a first offender aged 25 in receipt of £42 per fortnight in benefit, paid £20 per fortnight for his keep. The sheriff fined him £250 of which £80 had already been paid.

Sentence: on the court's calculation that his disposable income would be only £4.50, it would have taken the appellant a year to pay the fine which was excessive; and sentence quashed and fine of £80 substituted.

Dower v. Donnelly

1982 S.C.C.R. 465

(Lord Justice-General Emslie, Lords Cameron and Stott)

The appellant pled guilty to a charge of assault by headbutting, which was unprovoked and where the victim was uninjured. The appellant, who had been fined for a previous assault, earned £85 per week. The sheriff imposed 60 days' imprisonment.

Sentence: although the assault was unprovoked, there was no injury and the appellant deserved one more chance of reforming his behaviour before imposing a custodial sentence; and sentence quashed and £150 fine substituted.

9.3.4 Assault by hounding.

Kay v. Allan

(1978) S.C.C.R. Supp. 188

(Lord Justice-General Emslie, Lords Cameron and Avonside)

The appellant was convicted of assault by setting a dog on a boy aged nine which chased and bit him on the wrist and thigh without breaking the skin. The sheriff fined him £150.

Sentence: the £150 fine was harsh and oppressive, being out of proportion to the nature of the event; and sentence quashed and a fine of £25 substituted.

9.3.5   Assault by kicking to the head.

Dick v. *Jessop*
1989 S.C.C.R. 258
(Lords Brand, Murray and Sutherland)

A 25-year-old in employment who had no previous convictions for assault nor had received a custodial sentence was convicted of assaulting a man to his injury by repeatedly kicking him on the head and body while he was lying on the ground. He was sentenced to two months' imprisonment.

Sentence: the appellant had not previously committed a crime of violence nor received a custodial sentence; he had been in employment for five years which he would lose if imprisoned; the sentence was quashed and a fine of £500 imposed.

McCardle v. *Douglas*
1989 S.C.C.R. 262
(Lords Brand, Murray and Sutherland)

A 17-year-old in employment who had no previous convictions for assault nor had received a custodial sentence pled guilty to assaulting a man by kicking him while he was lying on the ground, resulting in injuries to his head. He was sentenced to 30 days' detention.

Sentence: the appellant had no record of violence nor received a custodial sentence; he was in employment; the sentence was quashed and a compensation order of £200 imposed.

9.3.6   Assault by police officer.

Gibson v. *Tudhope*
1986 S.C.C.R. 508
(Lord Justice-Clerk Ross, Lords Avonside and Hunter)

A police officer was convicted of assaulting a youth in the back of a police van, striking his head against the side of the van and striking him on the knee. The knee was injured. He was fined £500.

Sentence: upheld.

9.3.7 Assault by punching and kicking.

McCurdy v. *MacKinnon*
1987 S.C.C.R. 267
(Lord Justice-General Emslie, Lords Grieve and Brand)

A 17-year-old was convicted of punching and kicking a 15 year-old boy. He had been fined £10 for a previous assault and was sentenced to three months' detention.

Sentence: the sheriff was well-entitled to take the view that the assault was a vicious and unprovoked one on a 15-year-old boy to his injury and that a custodial sentence was the only way in which this kind of offence ought to be dealt with and the sentence was upheld.

Ferguson v. *Lowe*
1989 S.C.C.R. 281
(Lords Brand, Coulsfield and Milligan)

A 17-year-old in employment with no previous convictions was convicted of assaulting a bus driver by knocking him down and repeatedly punching and kicking him. He was sentenced to 60 days' detention.

Sentence: upheld.

9.3.8 Assault by throwing acid.

Modiak v. *H.M. Advocate*
1992 S.C.C.R. 572
(Lord Justice-General Hope, Lords Allanbridge and Cowie)

A man pled guilty to throwing sulphuric acid at his wife causing devastating injuries, completely destroying her appearance and leaving her sightless. He was sentenced to 20 years' imprisonment.

Sentence: upheld.

9.3.9   Assault by throwing tumbler.

Steele v. *MacKinnon*
1982 S.C.C.R. 19
(Lord Justice-Clerk Wheatley, Lords Hunter and Dunpark)

The appellant was convicted of assaulting a barmaid by throwing a tumbler at her. The sheriff sentenced him to three months' imprisonment in view of the potentially serious nature of the assault and the appellant's record which included four assaults for which fines of up to £25 had been imposed.

Sentence: the previous offences could not have been of any great severity judging from the level of the fines; a custodial sentence was not merited for the appellant, who had a wife and four children, was in employment and had never been to prison before; and sentence quashed and £100 fine substituted.

9.3.10   Assault on child.

General. In order to give as much protection as the courts can to very young children, anyone who assaults a child to his or her injury or severe injury must expect severe punishment at the hands of the courts.[2]

Practice.

Walker v. *H.M. Advocate*
1987 S.C.C.R. 345
(Lord Justice-General Emslie, Lords Kincraig and Cullen)

A man of low intelligence left in charge of an ill and irritable nine-month-old child was convicted of assaulting him to his severe injury. He was sentenced to four years' imprisonment.

Sentence: as the appellant was left in a situation where there was nobody capable of restraining him, the sentence was quashed and three years' imprisonment substituted.

C. v. *Lowe*
1990 S.C.C.R. 755
(Lords Wylie, McDonald and Brand)

A man pled guilty to assaulting two children, aged 10 and seven years, by removing the clothing of one and striking them with his hands and with an electric cable to their injury. He was sentenced to four months' imprisonment. He had served two months by the time of the appeal.

Sentence: it was in the interests of the children that when the appellant returned home he should be under the supervision of the social work department; the sentence was quashed and two years' probation imposed.

9.3.11   Assault on prosecution witness.

Furlong v. H.M. Advocate
1988 S.C.C.R. 452
(Lord Justice-Clerk Ross, Lords Avonside and Kincraig)

After a person had been convicted in a trial, he assaulted a prosecution witness as they left the court building by leaning against her and twisting his foot on her foot. He was sentenced to two years' imprisonment.

Sentence: the spontaneity of the action made no difference; it was quite intolerable that a person who had been tried on an offence should assault witnesses who had given evidence against him; the offence was an extremely serious one and the sentence was upheld.

9.3.12   Assault on spouse.

Pearson v. H.M. Advocate
1990 S.C.C.R. 125
See para. 9.3.17.

McMillan v. H.M. Advocate
1991 S.C.C.R. 20
(Lord Justice-Clerk Ross, Lords Morton of Shuna and Brand)

A first offender pled guilty to choking his wife with a piece of cable so that she became unconscious, to her injury and the danger of her life. He was in employment and had left the area where his wife lived. He was sentenced to three years' imprisonment.

Sentence: the offence was a very serious one but it was one which was unlikely to happen again; the circumstances were very special; the offence arose in a domestic situation and the appellant had taken steps to remove himself from that situation; the sentence was quashed and a community service order imposed.

9.3.13   Assault on water bailiff.

Mays v. *Brown*
1988 S.C.C.R. 549
(Lords Brand, Morison and Weir)

A man was convicted of assaulting a water bailiff by throwing a lamp at him. He was fined £250.

Sentence: it was notorious that poaching on a large scale was being carried on nowadays and that those such as water bailiffs whose duty it was to enforce the law were being subjected to dangerous abuse; the fine which was inadequate was quashed and a fine of £500 imposed.

9.3.14   Assault on woman by stranger.

McQuarrie v. *H.M. Advocate*
1988 S.C.C.R. 209
(Lords Brand, Prosser and Kincraig)

A man was convicted of assaulting a 19-year-old woman who was a total stranger to him in a ladies' toilet by punching and kicking her to her injury. He was sentenced to one year's imprisonment.

Sentence: upheld; the sentence was certainly not excessive and might well be described as unduly lenient.

9.3.15   Assault with glass.

Leslie v. *H.M. Advocate*
1992 S.C.C.R. 580
(Lords Cowie, Weir and Kincraig)

A 24-year-old was convicted of an assault in a public house involving striking a glass from which the victim was drinking into the face of the victim to severe injury and permanent disfigurement. He was sentenced to 18 months' imprisonment.

Sentence: while the sheriff was entitled to impose a custodial sentence, taking into account the appellant's good background, his lack of material previous convictions and the fact that he had served the equivalent of a six-month sentence, the sentence was quashed and community service of 240 hours and a compensation order of £1,500 were imposed.

McKay v. *H.M. Advocate*
1992 S.C.C.R. 584
(Lords Cowie, Weir and Kincraig)

A 40-year-old first offender was convicted of an assault at a dance, using a glass in his hand to strike the victim in the face, to severe injury and permanent disfigurement. He was sentenced to 15 months' imprisonment.

Sentence: upheld; this was a deliberate assault with a glass and although this was undoubtedly a severe sentence, it was not excessive.

9.3.16 Assault with intent to ravish.

Barbour v. *H.M. Advocate*
1982 S.C.C.R. 195
(Lord Stewart)

The appellant was convicted of abduction with intent to ravish and of two charges of assault with intent to ravish, all arising out of the same incident. He had a previous conviction for rape and one for assault with intent to ravish.

Sentence: 10 years' imprisonment.

9.3.17 Assault with knife.

Cairns v. *H.M. Advocate*
(1973) S.C.C.R. Supp. 44
(Lord Justice-Clerk Wheatley, Lords Milligan and Kissen)

An eight-year-old girl assaulted a 10-year-old girl by kicking her and stabbing her with a knife to her severe injury. The sheriff ordered her to be detained for 18 months under s. 57(2) of the Children and Young Persons (Scotland) Act 1937, as amended by the Social Work (Scotland) Act 1968.

Sentence: the question was whether the appropriate treatment for the girl was domiciliary or custodial; the interests of justice could best be served by providing for domiciliary treatment for the girl; and sentence quashed and three years' probation with the added condition of attendance at a hospital out-patient department of child and family psychiatry substituted.

Hart v. *H.M. Advocate*
1981 S.C.C.R. 286
(Lord Justice-General Emslie, Lords Avonside and Jauncey)

The appellant pled guilty to two charges of assault with a knife in which the injuries inflicted were not serious. He had one previous conviction for assault two years earlier when he was fined £100. He was sentenced to three years' detention in a young offenders institution.

Sentence: upheld; assaults with knives to injury were serious offences and this sentence was at the very bottom end of the scale of sentences appropriate for such offences.

Pearson v. *H.M. Advocate*
1990 S.C.C.R. 125
(Lords Wylie, Morison and Brand)

A first offender pled guilty to three assaults on his wife. The first two involved punching and kicking; the third was an assault with a knife to injury and permanent disfigurement. He was fined on the first two charges and sentenced to 15 months' imprisonment on the third.

Sentence: this was a domestic issue, the parties were now divorced and the assault was completely out of character; the sentence of imprisonment was quashed and 18 months' probation imposed.

9.3.18 Indecent assault.

General. The appeal court has stressed that it is always inclined to take a serious view of an offence of assault of an indecent nature on a young girl.[3]

Practice.

Cluness v. *Allan*
1984 S.C.C.R. 205
(Lord Justice-Clerk Wheatley, Lords Stott and Brand)

A 16-year-old first offender pled guilty to assaulting a 16-year-old girl by knocking her to the ground, lying on top of her, attempting to kiss her, fondling her breasts on top of her clothing and attempting to remove her trousers. He was sentenced to three months' detention.

Sentence: as the appellant was only 16, was in employment, had no previous convictions and had made a good impression on the social worker, the sentence was quashed and 12 months' probation imposed.

Penman v. *McPhail*
1987 S.C.C.R. 563
(Lord Justice-General Emslie, Lords Brand and Kincraig)

A sheriff disregarded the recommendation contained in the social enquiry report that a man who had pled guilty to indecent assault should be placed on probation and instead imposed a fine of £500.

Sentence: upheld.

Mitchell v. *Carmichael*
1988 S.C.C.R. 222
(Lords Grieve, Wylie and Sutherland)

A 23-year-old first offender pled guilty to indecently assaulting a 16-year-old girl. He had approached her in the street, fondled her, pulled her to the ground and placed his hand inside her trousers and blouse. He was sentenced to 60 days' imprisonment.

Sentence: quashed and a £500 fine imposed.

9.4 Breach of the peace

9.4.1 Football match.

McGivern v. *Jessop*
1988 S.C.C.R. 511
(Lords Brand, McDonald and Wylie)

A 19-year-old with one previous conviction for breach of the peace was convicted of breach of the peace by taunting rival football supporters, shouting and swearing, as groups of supporters were leaving a football ground after a match. He was sentenced to three months' detention.

Sentence: upheld; conduct of this kind was liable to lead to very serious consequences and must be severely discouraged.

9.4.2 Inconsiderate driving.

Craig v. *Herron*
(1976) S.C.C.R. Supp. 152
(Lord Justice-General Emslie, Lords Johnston and Avonside)

The appellant drove a taxi in front of another car, forcing it to stop, and then lectured the other driver calling him an idiot. The magistrate fined him £15.

Sentence: the offence was technical and trivial; and sentence quashed and fine of £5 substituted.

9.4.3 Swearing at police officers.

Worsfold v. *Walkingshaw*
1987 S.C.C.R. 17
(Lord Justice-Clerk Ross, Lords Robertson and Dunpark)

The appellant swore at police officers and was fined £100.

Sentence: swearing at police officers was reprehensible and the sheriff was entitled to impose a fine but it should bear a proper relationship to the charge; the fine was quashed and a £25 fine imposed.

9.4.4 Throwing lighted firework.

McLean v. *McNaughton*
1984 S.C.C.R. 319
(Lord Justice-General Emslie, Lord Justice-Clerk Wheatley and Lord Ross)

A 16-year-old first offender pled guilty to committing a breach of the peace by throwing a lighted firework which exploded on a bus. Two charges of vandalism committed the day before the breach of the peace were also before the court. He was sentenced to three months' detention.

Sentence: the breach of the peace was serious and could not be treated as an isolated, out of character incident, and the sentence was upheld.

9.5 Child kidnapping

Nicolson v. *H.M. Advocate*

1991 S.C.C.R. 606

(Lord Justice-General Hope, Lords Allanbridge and Brand)

A 36-year-old woman pled guilty to stealing a three-month-old baby from its pram in its grandparents' garden. She had been pregnant, miscarried and then had a phantom pregnancy. She told others that she had had twins, one of whom had died and the other of whom was in hospital. She travelled from Oban to Dumbarton, followed the grandparents and took the child. The child was recovered within a few hours. She was sentenced to 15 months' imprisonment by the Lord Justice-Clerk.

Sentence: upheld; the crime of child stealing was a very serious one, any sentence must take account of its gravity and it was the duty of the court to deter those tempted to resort to child stealing or kidnapping; the court had to be particularly vigilant in these cases to balance the public interest in the suppression of crime against the needs of the individual and in particular the need for rehabilitation; a case of deliberate and pre-meditated child stealing would inevitably attract a more severe sentence than one where the act was done suddenly on impulse under severe stress; in the latter case a non-custodial sentence might be appropriate but in the former case a custodial sentence would almost always be necessary to punish the offender and to deter others.[4]

9.6 Conspiracy

Reid v. *H.M. Advocate*

1990 S.C.C.R. 83

(Lord Justice-General Hope, Lords Brand and Cowie)

Two appellants were convicted of a conspiracy to further the purposes of the Ulster Defence Association by criminal means and were sentenced to 12 and 16 years' imprisonment respectively.

Sentences: upheld.

9.7 Consumer credit

Currys Ltd. v. *Jessop*

1988 S.C.C.R. 447

(Lords Grieve, Avonside and Kincraig)

A large retail company pled guilty to advertising credit terms as including nothing to pay for three months; in fact, interest would run for the first three months and be payable thereafter. They were fined £1,500.

Sentence: upheld.

9.8 Contempt of court

General. The maximum penalty which may be imposed by way of imprisonment for contempt of court in Scottish proceedings is now two years.[5] In the case of a person under 21 years of age or who had not previously served a custodial sentence who was found to be in contempt of court, it would be incompetent to order an immediate sentence of detention or imprisonment.[6]

Practice.

Wylie v. H.M. Advocate
1966 S.L.T. 149
(Lord Justice-General Clyde, Lords Guthrie and Migdale)

Two Crown witnesses entered the witness box in the High Court of Justiciary but refused either to take the oath or to give evidence. They refused to give any explanation or justification. Each was sentenced to three years' imprisonment.

Sentence: upheld; a lesser sentence could not fail to be anything but an encouragement to others to seek to evade their plain duty to society; in future cases it might be necessary to impose a still more severe sentence.

Manson, Petitioner
(1977) S.C.C.R. Supp. 176
(Lord Justice-General Emslie, Lords Cameron and Johnston)

After a fellow prisoner had been stabbed to death, the petitioner was sentenced to three years' imprisonment for contempt of court as a witness in the ensuing murder trial.

Sentence: a sentence of imprisonment for contempt of court at that time, as opposed to a sentence for imprisonment for crime, carried no eligibility for parole; accordingly, where the sentence of imprisonment for contempt was ordered to take effect after a sentence for a crime, the prisoner would not be eligible for parole for either sentence; and sentence quashed and two years' imprisonment substituted.[7]

Hislop, Petitioner
1986 S.C.C.R. 268
(Lord Justice-Clerk Ross, Lords Robertson and Dunpark)

A defence witness in a High Court drugs trial, in which the accused had lodged a special defence of incrimination naming William Rodgers, admitted in her evidence obtaining drugs from William Rodgers and from other persons whom she refused to name. She was found to be in contempt of court and sentenced to nine months' imprisonment.

Sentence: upheld, having regard to the fact that this was a flagrant contempt of court.

Adams, Petitioner
1987 S.C.C.R. 650
(Lord Justice-General Emslie, Lords Grieve and Kincraig)

The news editor of Radio Clyde received a message from an experienced freelance court reporter which included a statement that a plea of guilty to culpable homicide by an accused person in a murder trial had been rejected. The message was broadcast and the trial had to be abandoned. The editor and the reporter were found to be in contempt of court and fined £20,000 and £5,000 respectively.

Sentence: the report which was of a specialist nature was submitted by an experienced source; it was difficult to identify any degree of culpability on the part of the editor which ought to be reflected in a penalty and that penalty was quashed.

Smith, Petitioner
1987 S.C.C.R. 726
(Lord Justice-General Emslie, Lords Grieve and Brand)

A Crown witness in a High Court trial refused to answer a question as to who his accomplice had been and the trial had to be abandoned. He was found to be in contempt of court and sentenced to three years' imprisonment.

Sentence: the sentence was incompetent in view of s. 15(2) of the Contempt of Court Act 1981; it was quashed and a sentence of 18 months' imprisonment was imposed.

9.9 Counterfeit banknotes

General. The appeal court has indicated that offences in relation to counterfeit banknotes are always serious because it is of the greatest importance that the public should have confidence in the currency of the country.[8]

Practice.

Taylor v. Tudhope
1986 S.C.C.R. 77
(Lord Justice-General Emslie, Lords Grieve and Cowie)

The appellant was convicted of possessing six counterfeit £20 banknotes and sentenced to six months' imprisonment.

Sentence: the crime of possession of counterfeit currency notes has to be treated as a serious one but the six months' imprisonment was quashed and three months' imprisonment imposed.

McLeod v. Allan
1986 S.C.C.R. 666
(Lord Justice-Clerk Ross, Lords Robertson and McDonald)

An appellant, with no previous convictions for dishonesty, passed a counterfeit £50 note and was sentenced to three months' imprisonment. The offence was said to be becoming rife in Edinburgh and the maximum sentence was six months' imprisonment.

Sentence: upheld.

9.10 Culpable homicide

Duff v. H.M. Advocate
1983 S.C.C.R. 461
(Lord Justice-General Emslie, Lords Cameron and Dunpark)

Charged with murdering his aunt by striking, strangling and stabbing her, the nephew pled guilty to culpable homicide due to diminished responsibility, which plea was accepted by the Crown. Taking the view that there could be no assurance that he would not act similarly in the future, the trial judge sentenced him to life imprisonment.

Sentence: upheld; the trial judge did not err in the exercise of his discretion and the sentence was not excessive but was the best possible sentence from the point of view of both the offender and the public, being subject to periodic review.

Mowles v. H.M. Advocate
1986 S.C.C.R. 117
(Lord Justice-General Emslie, Lords Brand and Kincraig)

On being asked by a friend to help to remove two men from his house, the appellant reluctantly agreed and took with him his brother's shotgun. When cocked this would discharge itself if knocked or dropped but it could not be fired by pressing the trigger. The appellant tried the trigger and believed the gun to be unloaded. He pointed the gun through the window of the house and someone took hold of the barrel, causing it to discharge and killing the deceased. He was sentenced to five years' imprisonment.

Sentence: in these highly special circumstances the sentence was excessive; it was quashed and, merely to reflect the original assault, a sentence of six months' imprisonment was imposed.

T. v. H.M. Advocate
1990 S.C.C.R. 540
(Lord Justice-Clerk Ross, Lords Wylie and Morison)

A woman was convicted of the culpable homicide of her two sons on the ground of diminished responsibility. She had set fire to their home. She was sentenced to 10 years' imprisonment.

Sentence: having considered the possibility of imposing a sentence of life imprisonment, the Court of Criminal Appeal concluded that it would not be an appropriate disposal in this case; it was important for the appellant to have a goal to which to look forward and she could only have such a goal if the sentence was one which permitted her to calculate an expected release date; the sentence was not excessive and was upheld.

K. v. *H.M. Advocate*
1991 S.C.C.R. 703
(Lord Justice-Clerk Ross, Lords Cameron and Grieve)

A 12-year-old child was convicted of the culpable homicide of a three-year-old girl. Psychiatric reports indicated that he was emotionally disturbed, that further behavioural problems were likely in the future and that continued assessment would be necessary. He was sentenced to be detained without limit of time.

Sentence: upheld; the sentence was competent and was in the best interests of both the appellant and the public.

Welsh v. *H.M. Advocate*
1992 S.C.C.R. 108
(Lord Justice-Clerk Ross, Lords Morison and Milligan)

The deceased was killed by three men assaulting him on a common stair. The appellant was convicted of culpable homicide and sentenced to 12 years' imprisonment.

Sentence: upheld.

Brodie v. *H.M. Advocate*
1992 S.C.C.R. 487
(Lord Justice-Clerk Ross, Lords Morison and Penrose)

An appellant was convicted of culpable homicide by driving recklessly while under the influence of alcohol to such an extent as to be incapable of having proper control of a car. He had a previous conviction for causing death by reckless driving. He was sentenced to eight years' imprisonment.

Sentence: upheld.

9.11 Drugs

9.11.1 Supply.

General. The appeal court has warned that those who traffic in drugs can only expect severe sentences at the hands of the courts.[9] Trafficking in Class A drugs is regarded as a very serious offence which the courts will do their utmost to suppress.[10]

Supply to friend.

McWilliams v. H.M. Advocate
1985 S.C.C.R. 419
(Lord Justice-General Emslie, Lords Grieve and Kincraig)

A drug addict shared half a gramme of heroin with a fellow-addict when the latter had none and was suffering severely from withdrawal symptoms. He was sentenced to three years' imprisonment which he argued must be excessive simply for sharing his own fix with a friend.

Sentence: upheld, being a very low sentence for the offence.

Gibson v. H.M. Advocate
1992 S.C.C.R. 885
(Lord Justice-Clerk Ross, Lords Grieve and Wylie)

A woman pled guilty to supplying cannabis resin and to being in possession of £35 of cannabis resin. She was a first offender and the supply was to friends only. She was sentenced to nine months' imprisonment on the supply charge.

Sentence: while offences such as supplying drugs should attract severe sentences, the court must always have regard to the circumstances of any particular case and insufficient weight had been placed on the appellant being a first offender, on the quantity of the drugs involved being very small and on the supply taking place among friends; sentence quashed and 180 hours' community service imposed.

Supply to prisoner.

Kerr v. H.M. Advocate
1991 S.C.C.R. 774
(Lord Justice-General Hope, Lords Allanbridge and Cowie)

A 26-year-old man was convicted of supplying £7 worth of cannabis resin (Class B) and nine buprenorphine tablets (Class C) to a prisoner he was visiting. He was sentenced to two years' and 18 months' imprisonment respectively, to run concurrently.

Sentence: upheld; the supply of drugs to prisoners was a well-known evil which required to be dealt with severely when detected.

9.11.2 Supply and possession with intent to supply.
(Class B).

Miller v. *H.M. Advocate*
1985 S.C.C.R. 314
(Lord Justice-General Emslie, Lords Cameron and Brand)

A 33-year-old mother of four children of whom three, including a ten-month-old baby were her personal responsibility, was convicted of supplying cannabis and of possessing cannabis with intent to supply it. The cannabis supplied was worth about £10 and the cannabis possessed was valued at between £360 and £600. She was sentenced to four years' imprisonment.

Sentence: for the sole reason of the effect of the imprisonment upon the future of the young children, including in particular the baby, the sentence was quashed and one of three years' imprisonment imposed.

9.11.3 Offering to supply.
(Class B)

McNab v. *H.M. Advocate*
1986 S.C.C.R. 230
(Lord Justice-Clerk Ross, Lords Robertson and Avonside)

Someone who offered to supply cannabis resin with a street value of £40 to two police officers in a public house was sentenced to nine months' imprisonment.

Sentence: upheld; for an offence of this nature the sentence could not possibly be regarded as excessive.

9.11.4 Concerned in supply.

General. The appeal court has indicated that there is no room for the view that being concerned in a drug activity is any less serious than the activity itself.[11]

Practice.
(Class B).

McIntosh v. *H.M. Advocate*
1986 J.C. 169; 1986 S.C.C.R. 496; 1987 S.L.T. 296
(Lord Justice-Clerk Ross, Lords Robertson and Sutherland)

The appellant was sentenced to seven years' imprisonment for being concerned in the supply of cannabis resin.

Sentence: upheld; the evidence that he had £3,000 in a bag and the use of a new Mercedes car suggested that he was concerned in the supplying of controlled drugs to a very material extent.

9.11.5   Possession with intent to supply.

General. It has repeatedly been said in the courts that a serious view will be taken of offences of possession of controlled drugs with intent to supply them and that if, despite these warnings, persons commit these offences they must accept the consequences.[12]

Practice.

(Class A).

Cunningham v. H.M. Advocate
1988 S.C.C.R. 514
(Lord Justice-Clerk Ross, Lords McDonald and Wylie)

The appellant pled guilty to possessing a deal of heroin and other drugs worth £25 with intent to supply to another, the intended transaction being non-commercial. He was sentenced to six months' imprisonment.

Sentence: upheld; any offence of this kind, whether the supply was on a commercial basis or not, was a serious matter and one which contributed to the use of drugs by others.

(Class B).

Donnelly v. H.M. Advocate
1984 S.C.C.R. 93
(Lord Justice-General Emslie, Lords Cameron and Grieve)

The appellant pled guilty to possessing 36 grammes of cannabis resin with intent to supply, the street value being between £273 and £400. He was sentenced to 18 months' imprisonment and £1,047 found hidden in his house was ordered to be forfeited.

Sentence: upheld; those who traffic in drugs can only expect severe sentences at the hands of the court.

Varley v. H.M. Advocate
1985 S.C.C.R. 55
(Lord Justice-General Emslie, Lords Cameron and Brand)

A musician pled guilty to possessing 666.96 grammes of cannabis with a street value of £2,500 with intent to supply it to others. He claimed that he only intended to supply it to a limited circle of friends. He had two minor previous drugs convictions and was sentenced to four years' imprisonment.

Sentence: upheld, it being well-known that the High Court of Justiciary was determined to pass severe sentences for possession of drugs, whether Class A or B, with intent to supply others.

Wright v. Houston
1987 S.C.C.R. 674
(Lord Justice-Clerk Ross, Lords Dunpark and McDonald)

The appellant was convicted on summary complaint of possessing cannabis resin with intent to supply it to another and of permitting cannabis to be smoked in his house. The value of the cannabis was £75. He had previously been imprisoned but had no previous drugs convictions. He was sentenced to 12 months' imprisonment on each charge, concurrent.

Sentence: upheld.

Hemphill v. H.M. Advocate
1989 S.C.C.R. 433
(Lord Justice-General Emslie, Lords Cowie and Clyde)

A man with no previous convictions for drug-related offences pled guilty to possessing 334 mg of cannabis resin with intent to supply it. He was sentenced to three years' imprisonment.

Sentence: upheld.

Hudson v. H.M. Advocate
1990 S.C.C.R. 200
(Lord Justice-General Hope, Lords Cowie and Morison)

A man pled guilty to possessing 426.48 grammes of cannabis resin with intent to supply to another. He said that he had purchased the drugs for himself and three friends while on holiday in Fife. He was sentenced to four years' imprisonment.

Sentence: upheld.

Lindsay v. *H.M. Advocate*
1992 S.C.C.R. 897
(Lords Allanbridge, Wylie and Kincraig)

A man pled guilty to possessing 46.449 grammes of cannabis resin with a street value of between £180 and £200 with intent to supply. He had a number of previous convictions, none for analogous offences. He was sentenced to 18 months' imprisonment.

Sentence: upheld; although the sentence was severe it was not excessive.

McMillan v. *H.M. Advocate*
1992 S.C.C.R. 900
(Lords Allanbridge, Wylie and Kincraig)

A woman was convicted of possessing amphetamine with a street value of between £70 and £105 with intent to supply. She was sentenced to six months' imprisonment.

Sentence: there were exceptional circumstances in that the appellant who had a good background report and a good record was living with a drug dealer and succumbed to the temptation of dealing in drugs to a very limited extent; sentence quashed and 200 hours' community service imposed.

9.11.6 Possession with intent to supply and offer to supply.

(Class A).

Mullady v. *H.M. Advocate*
1988 S.C.C.R. 113
(Lords Brand, Morison and Avonside)

A person with several previous convictions but none for drugs offences was convicted of possessing lysergide to a value of £100 with intent to supply it to others and with offering to supply it to another. He was sentenced to four years' detention on each charge, concurrent.

Sentence: a sentence of four years' imprisonment was the minimum sentence which was appropriate for trafficking in Class A drugs and the sentence was upheld.

9.11.7   Possession with intent to supply and possession.
(Classes B and A respectively).

Walker v. *H.M. Advocate*
1987 S.C.C.R. 379
(Lord Justice-Clerk Ross, Lords McDonald and Wylie)

The appellant was convicted of possessing heroin and of possessing Class B drugs with intent to supply them. She had two previous convictions for possessing drugs and was sentenced to one year's imprisonment on each charge, the sentences to run consecutively.

Sentence: the sentences imposed on someone with previous convictions for the unlawful possession of drugs was inadequate and the sentences were quashed and two years' imprisonment imposed on each charge, to run concurrently.

9.11.8   Possession.
(Class A).

Hoy v. *McLeod*
1983 S.C.C.R. 149
(Lord Justice-General Emslie, Lords Cameron and Avonside)

A 34-year-old man pled guilty to possession of heroin and cannabis. He was already on probation for possession of controlled drugs and was sentenced to the maximum on summary conviction of 12 months' imprisonment on the heroin charge, with three months' imprisonment concurrent on the cannabis charge.

Sentence: the only question was whether by imposing the maximum sentence the sheriff had gone too far too fast; a shorter sentence would suffice and the sentence on the heroin charge was quashed and six months' imprisonment substituted.

Ramsey v. *H.M. Advocate*
1984 S.C.C.R. 409
(Lord Justice-General Emslie, Lords Cameron and Grieve)

On pleading guilty to possession of small amounts of heroin on two occasions, the trial judge, observing that he treated this as a serious case of drug addiction, sentenced the offender to four years' imprisonment.

Sentence: drug addiction was not a crime; the offender was in possession of what amounted for him to only one-and-a-half days' supply of heroin; and the sentence was reduced to two years' imprisonment. [13]

Campbell v. *H.M. Advocate*
1986 S.C.C.R. 403
(Lord Justice-Clerk Ross, Lords Dunpark and McDonald)

For being in possession of three grams of cocaine, the appellant, who had five previous convictions relating to Class B drugs, was sentenced to three years' imprisonment.

Sentence: upheld.

Money v. *H.M. Advocate*
1988 S.C.C.R. 127
(Lord Justice-General Emslie, Lords Brand and Allanbridge)

A man was convicted of possessing 580 mg of heroin and was sentenced to 21 months' imprisonment.

Sentence: upheld; although the sentence was severe it was not excessive.

McCreadie v. *Walkingshaw*
1990 S.C.C.R. 761 (Lords Wylie, McDonald and Brand)

The appellant pled guilty to possessing 0.1 g of cocaine valued at £40 as well as cannabis resin and amphetamine. As this was the first occasion in the jurisdiction that a person had been found in possession of cocaine, the sheriff imposed a deterrent sentence of six months' imprisonment on that charge and 30 days' imprisonment concurrent on the others.

Sentence: upheld.

(Classes A and B).

Meighan v. *Jessop*
1989 S.C.C.R. 208
(Lord Justice-General Emslie, Lords Brand and Allanbridge)

Traces of heroin and disubstituted barbituric acid were found in the appellant's possession. Sentence was deferred for a year, during which time he was of good behaviour. He had obtained employment as a drugs counsellor. He was fined £150 and £50 respectively.

Sentence: the sheriff had taken all the factors into account in not imposing a custodial sentence and instead selecting relatively small fines, which were upheld.

Kennedy v. *H.M. Advocate*
1990 S.C.C.R. 417
(Lords Allanbridge, Cowie and Brand)

A man was convicted in the High Court of possessing lysergide and cannabis resin with a total value of £15. He was sentenced to 18 and nine months' imprisonment respectively, concurrent.

Sentence: the sentences were quashed and sentences of nine and four-and-a-half months' imprisonment respectively, concurrent, imposed.

(Class B).

Grundison v. *Brown*
1987 S.C.C.R. 186
(Lord Justice-General Emslie, Lords Grieve and Kincraig)

A first offender pled guilty to possessing 226 mg of cannabis resin with a value of 50p. He was fined £100.

Sentence: the sentence was quashed and an admonition substituted, with the warning that if the appellant was convicted again he could not expect a further admonition.

Simpson v. *Hamilton*
1988 S.C.C.R. 163
(Lords Brand, Prosser and Kincraig)

A first offender pled guilty to possessing a mixture of cannabis resin and tobacco weighing 1.1 gramme. He was fined £125.

Sentence: quashed and an admonition substituted.

Cleland v. *McLeod*
1988 S.C.C.R. 509
(Lords Brand, McDonald and Wylie)

Two first offenders were convicted of possessing 197 mg and 1.2 g respectively of cannabis resin and were each fined £125.

Sentence: upheld.

Kenmure v. *Lowe*
1990 S.C.C.R. 367
(Lords Allanbridge, Sutherland and McDonald)

A first offender pled guilty to possessing 1.17 grammes of cannabis resin and was fined £40.

Sentence: upheld.

Observed: Grundison v. *Brown* 1987 S.C.C.R. 186 and *Simpson* v. *Hamilton* 1988 S.C.C.R. 163 did not lay down any tariff. Each case must be considered on its own merits.

Isdale v. *Scott*
1991 S.C.C.R. 491
(Lords Cowie, Sutherland and McDonald)

The appellant pled guilty to being in possession of 28 grammes of cannabis resin. The sheriff told him that if the identity of his suppliers was revealed the disposal would be more lenient. The appellant gave an unknown name and a non-existent address. He was sentenced to 60 days' imprisonment.

Sentence: the provision of information about a drug supplier might be a mitigating factor in sentence but failure or refusal to give that information was not a reason for imposing a custodial sentence; the sentence was quashed and sentence was deferred for a year, when the appellant was admonished.

McQueen v. *Hingston*
1992 S.C.C.R. 92
(Lords Cowie, Weir and Prosser)

A car salesman with five children pled guilty to possessing 9.5 grammes of cannabis resin, admitting a number of previous convictions. He was sentenced to 60 days' imprisonment.

Sentence: quashed and a fine of £1,500 was substituted.

9.11.9   Importing and being concerned in importation.

General. Being concerned in a drug activity is no less serious than the activity itself.[14]

Practice.
(Class A).

Howarth v. H.M. Advocate (No. 2)

1992 S.C.C.R. 525

(Lord Justice-General Hope, Lords Allanbridge and Weir)

Three appellants were convicted of being concerned in the importation of half a metric ton of cocaine valued at £100m. One was sentenced to 25 years' imprisonment, the others to 15 years' imprisonment each.

Sentences: upheld; those who engage in the importation of Class A drugs must expect severe sentences; the length of the sentences must to some degree reflect the amount and value of the drugs involved.

(Class B).

MacNeil v. H.M. Advocate

1986 J.C. 146; 1986 S.C.C.R. 288; 1987 S.L.T. 244[15]

(Lord Justice-General Emslie, Lords Robertson and Brand)

The first two appellants were sentenced to 12 years' imprisonment, the second being fined £100,000 in addition, on charges of importing two-thirds of a ton of cannabis and possession of cannabis. The third appellant was convicted of being concerned in the importation of the cannabis and was sentenced to 10 years' imprisonment.

Sentence: importing prohibited drugs and possession of large quantities of controlled drugs with intent to supply them on a large scale were very serious matters calling for severe sentences and the sentences were upheld.

9.12   Embezzlement

Dolan v. H.M. Advocate

1986 S.C.C.R. 564

(Lord Justice-Clerk Ross, Lords Brand and Avonside)

A local authority accountant, embittered about lack of promotion, embezzled £23,728.43. The money was repaid. He was sentenced to 15 months' imprisonment.

Sentence: it was not necessary to impose a custodial sentence; this was a serious breach of trust and called for an appropriate punishment; the sentence was quashed and a £3,000 fine imposed.

9.13 Extortion

Rae v. *Donnelly*
1982 S.C.C.R. 148
(Lord Justice-Clerk Wheatley, Lords Hunter and Robertson)

The managing director of a company dismissed a pregnant employee on hearing that a foreman mechanic employed by the company was the father of the child. After proceedings for wrongful dismissal were brought, he asked the dismissed employee to drop the proceedings and the mechanic to resign or else he would tell the truth to her parents and to his wife. He was fined £1,000.

Sentence: upheld.

9.14 False accusations

Simpkins v. *H.M. Advocate*
1985 S.C.C.R. 30
(Lord Justice-General Emslie, Lords Cameron and Brand)

Two security officers falsely accused two boys of shoplifting. They detained the boys and articles allegedly stolen were produced to the police. The senior officer was sentenced to nine months' imprisonment and the other to six months, "the minimum effective to record the court's abhorrence of [their] conduct".

Sentence: upheld; it was a grave crime and plainly demanded a custodial sentence and the sentences imposed were not excessive.

9.15 Fire raising

Donaldson v. *H.M. Advocate*
1983 S.C.C.R. 216
(Lord Justice-Clerk Wheatley, Lords Hunter and Robertson)

A 19-year-old woman pled guilty to seven charges of fire raising. In medical reports she was described as highly dangerous and as likely to remain so for many years. She was sentenced to be detained for life.

Sentence: upheld.

9.16 Firearms

9.16.1 CS gas canister.

Donnelly v. *H.M. Advocate*
1988 S.C.C.R. 386
(Lords Brand, Allanbridge and Mayfield)

A 16-year-old first offender pled guilty to possession of a CS gas canister at a football match. He was sentenced to 18 months' detention.

Sentence: the sentence was inadequate; it was quashed and two years' detention imposed.

Ferguson v. *H.M. Advocate*
1991 S.C.C.R. 965
(Lords Allanbridge, Brand and Wylie)

The appellant was convicted of being in possession of a CS gas canister. He had earlier been going to a football match but had been unable to enter the ground. He was sentenced to 12 months' detention.

Sentence: upheld; those who go to football matches carrying weapons as described in s. 5(1) of the Firearms Act 1968 could only expect severe punishment.

9.16.2 Shotgun.

Wagstaff v. *Wilson*
1989 S.C.C.R. 322
(Lords Brand, Wylie and Grieve)

A married man with two children whose total family income was £93 per week in benefits pled guilty to possessing a shotgun in his home without a licence. He was fined £500.

Sentence: upheld; members of the public must be deterred from holding firearms without a certificate.

Wallace v. H.M. Advocate
1992 S.C.C.R. 439
(Lords Cowie, Mayfield and Marnoch)

An 18-year-old pled guilty to possessing a sawn-off shotgun which he said he had found a few days before it was discovered in his bedroom by his mother. He was sentenced to nine months' detention.

Sentence: upheld and the sheriff's views that only a custodial sentence was appropriate because of the gravity of the offence and that the courts ought to do all that they could to discourage people from keeping weapons endorsed.

9.17 Food and drugs

Alex Munro (Butchers) Ltd v. Carmichael
1990 S.C.C.R. 275
(Lord Justice-General Hope, Lords Wylie and Brand)

A company was convicted of selling a cooked chicken which had gone bad because it had been exposed for sale on successive days. It was fined £750.

Sentence: having regard to the nature of the offence and the size of the appellant's business, the sentence could not be described as excessive and it was upheld.

9.18 Fraud

9.18.1 Frauds by solicitor.

Jenkins v. H.M. Advocate
1984 S.C.C.R. 411
(Lord Justice-General Emslie, Lords Cameron and Grieve)

A solicitor pled guilty to obtaining £116,000 by making false applications for bridging loans. The money was used to assist two clients who had asked him to see if funds could be provided for property development. When these frauds were discovered by the bank, the solicitor obtained a further £109,000 from another bank by fraud in order to repay the first bank. In time he repaid the second bank with the help of friends who were reimbursed by the original clients. He was sentenced to 18 months' imprisonment.

Sentence: upheld, these being deliberate frauds committed by a professional man in the course of his duty, in whose word trust was constantly placed by the financial institutions with which he dealt.

9.18.2 Fraud and theft.

White v. *H.M. Advocate*
1987 S.C.C.R. 73
(Lord Justice-General Emslie, Lords Robertson and Avonside)

An architect appointed to supervise repair work on houses for which a repair grant was payable by a district council pled guilty to the theft of £9,371.33 of grant which should have been paid over to the contractors and to defrauding the council of £10,800 by making grant claims for work which had not been done. He had prospects of being able to repay the money. He was sentenced to 18 months' imprisonment. The money was repaid by the time of the appeal.

Sentence: it made a difference that the money had been repaid and that the appellant was attempting to re-establish himself; the sentence was quashed and a fine of £4,000 substituted.

Dolan v. *H.M. Advocate* 1986 S.C.C.R. 564 followed.

9.18.3 Obtaining legal aid by fraud.

McGhee v. *H.M. Advocate*
1987 S.C.C.R. 702
(Lord Justice-Clerk Ross, Lords Dunpark and McDonald)

An appellant pled guilty on indictment to obtaining legal aid by fraud in respect that he had failed to disclose that he owned a property valued at £75,000. He was fined £5,000. The maximum fine for the corresponding summary statutory offence was £1,000.

Sentence: the fine was quashed and a fine of £1,000 imposed.

9.18.4 Obtaining benefits by fraud.

MacRae v. *H.M. Advocate*
1987 S.C.C.R. 712
(Lord Justice-Clerk Ross, Lords Dunpark and McDonald)

A 52-year-old first offender obtained £3,500 by fraudulently obtaining supplementary benefit over a two-year period by failing to declare that his wife was employed. He was sentenced to nine months' imprisonment.

Sentence: this was a very blatant fraud and the sheriff was fully justified in forming the view that only a custodial disposal was appropriate and the sentence was upheld.

9.18.5 Falsifying odometers.

McLean v. *H.M. Advocate*

1991 S.C.C.R. 972

(Lords Allanbridge, Brand and Wylie)

A car dealer pled guilty to selling seven cars with falsified odometers. The price of each car was increased by an average of about £700. He was imprisoned for nine months.

Sentence: upheld; it was notorious that many car dealers carried out this type of fraud and the public interest demanded that a severe view must be taken of such cases.

9.19 Glue-sniffing kits

General. The Court of Criminal Appeal has indicated that it wishes to make it perfectly clear that those who are convicted of the "wicked crime" of supplying glue-sniffing kits to children may expect severe sentences at the hands of the High Court.[16]

Practice.

Khaliq v. *H.M. Advocate*

1984 S.C.C.R. 212

(Lord Justice-General Emslie, Lords Cameron and Stott)

Two shopkeepers pled guilty to supplying glue-sniffing kits to children to the danger of their health and lives. The trial judge sentenced them to three years' imprisonment.

Sentence: as the appellants had genuinely believed that they were not committing a crime and their pleas of guilty had spared the children the further pain of giving evidence, the sentences were reduced to two years' imprisonment.

Observed: persons convicted of this "wicked crime" in the future might expect more severe sentences at the hands of the High Court.

Ulhaq v. *H.M. Advocate*
1990 S.C.C.R. 593; 1991 S.L.T. 614
(Lord Justice-General Hope, Lords Cowie and Kirkwood)

The appellant was convicted of selling solvents to a number of people in their twenties in the knowledge that they were intended for inhalation. He was sentenced to two years' imprisonment.

Sentence: the ages of the purchasers were a factor which ought not to have been left out of account in assessing the gravity of the offence; the supply did not involve the sale of kits but only the solvents themselves in their normal containers; the sentence was quashed and 200 hours' community service substituted.

Observed: the Court of Criminal Appeal indicated that it wished to make it clear that it regarded this as an exceptional case and that severe sentences involving periods of imprisonment must continue to be expected, especially where children were the recipients of the supply.

9.20 Health and safety at work

Briggs Amasco Ltd. and Anr. v. *Smith*
1981 S.C.C.R. 274
(Lord Justice-General Emslie, Lords Avonside and Jauncey)

A company of roofing contractors and their departmental manager pled guilty to breaches of the Health and Safety at Work etc. Act 1974 by requiring their employees to work on an unfenced flat roof eight metres above ground level, the sole access to which was by a timber ladder with a fractured stile. The manager had visited the site and had received complaints about the absence of fencing and the state of the ladder. The company had 10 analogous previous convictions for which it had been fined sums ranging from £10 to £1,000. The sheriff imposed on the company the maximum fine of £1,000 and on the manager £500, one-half of the maximum.

Sentence: (1) in view of the size of the company and its large number of employees, the steps that it took to promote safety and the previous Scottish fines being in a range from £10 to £350, the fine was reduced to £500; and (2) as the manager's culpability was not such as to merit a fine appropriate to an offence of a grave order, his fine was reduced to £100.

Kvaerner Govan Ltd. v. *H.M. Advocate*
1992 S.C.C.R. 10
(Lords Cowie, Grieve and Brand)

A shipbuilding company was convicted of failing to provide their employees with safe access and proper instructions regarding access, resulting in the death of a foreman. The company had an analogous previous conviction. A fine of £20,000 was imposed.

Sentence: upheld; there was no yardstick by which one could test whether the fine was excessive except by considering whether the sheriff had had regard to all of the relevant circumstances.

9.21 Murder

9.21.1 Murder. A person convicted of murder must be sentenced to imprisonment for life. If a person convicted of murder is under the age of 18 years, instead of being sentenced to life imprisonment, he must be sentenced to be detained without limit of time. He is liable to be detained in such place and under such conditions as the Secretary of State may direct. A person convicted of murder who has attained the age of 18 years but is under the age of 21 years must be sentenced to be detained in a young offenders institution and is liable to be detained for life.[17]

On sentencing any person convicted of murder, a judge may make a recommendation as to the minimum period which should elapse before the Secretary of State releases that person on licence. When making a recommendation the judge must state his reasons for so recommending. It is competent to appeal against a recommendation; the recommendation is deemed part of the sentence passed on conviction.[18]

9.21.2 Attempted murder.

W. v. *H.M. Advocate*
1989 S.C.C.R. 461
(Lord Justice-Clerk Ross, Lords Wylie and Murray)

A 22-year-old woman was convicted of attempting to murder her two-year-old daughter by holding a pillow over her face. She was sentenced to five years' imprisonment.

Sentence: this was a highly unusual case in that apart from on this occasion no criticism was made of the way in which the appellant cared for her child; the sentence was quashed and three years' probation imposed.

9.22   Offensive weapon

9.22.1   Offensive weapon and other offence. A sentence for having an offensive weapon may be in addition to any other penalty and prison sentences may be made consecutive. Where a person pled guilty to assault by striking a man with a razor and to having an offensive weapon, namely the razor, in a public place, he was sentenced to one year's detention on each charge, the sentences to run consecutively. Although it was argued that the two offences were really one and that therefore the sentences ought to have been concurrent, the appeal court disagreed and viewed the two sentences as separate. The statutory offence was committed as soon as the offender took the razor to a public place and could have been committed whether or not the assault had taken place.[19]

9.22.2   Knife.

O'Rourke v. *Lockhart*
1984 S.C.C.R. 322
(Lord Justice-General Emslie, Lord Justice-Clerk Wheatley and Lord Ross)

Having been assaulted by others, the appellant went home, collected a knife and took it to a street where he brandished it at passers-by. He was sentenced to 60 days' imprisonment.

Sentence: the sheriff had paid too little attention to the antecedents of the offence; the sentence was quashed and a £250 fine substituted.

Smith v. *Wilson*
1987 S.C.C.R. 191
(Lord Justice-General Emslie, Lords Grieve and Kincraig)

A first offender pled guilty to having a flick knife with him in a car. He was sentenced to three months' imprisonment.

Sentence: upheld.

Jacobs v. *Wilson*
1989 S.C.C.R. 9
(Lords McDonald, Morison and Weir)

A first offender pled guilty to having a butcher's knife with a ten-inch blade in a street at 4 am. He claimed that he had been chased by two youths, had run into his house and come out with the knife and that the youths had run off. He was sentenced to three months' imprisonment.

Sentence: a judge should not fetter his discretion by invariably imposing a custodial sentence for possession of an offensive weapon and the sentence was quashed and 120 hours' community service imposed.

Smith v. *Wilson* 1987 S.C.C.R. 191 was distinguished because the weapon here was not *per se* an offensive weapon and because it was originally acquired for defensive purposes only.

Kane v. *H.M. Advocate*
1988 S.C.C.R. 585
(Lord Justice-Clerk Ross, Lords Dunpark and McDonald)

The appellant was in possession of a Stanley knife fixed in the exposed position when searched by police officers following his detention on a charge of theft. He was sentenced to four months' detention.

Sentence: upheld.

9.22.3   Piece of wood.

Addison v. *MacKinnon*
1983 S.C.C.R. 52
(Lord Justice-Clerk Wheatley, Lords Robertson and Stott)

A first offender waved a four-foot-long piece of wood with a jagged edge in a street while shouting gang slogans. He was described in the social enquiry report as a quiet and pleasant boy, although the sheriff formed a contrary impression of him. He was sentenced to three months' detention.

Sentence: the sheriff had not given sufficient consideration to the fact that the appellant was a first offender and had over-reacted in view of the general circumstances which prevailed in the area; the sentence of detention was quashed and a fine of £100 imposed.

9.23 Perjury

General. Considerations of general deterrence in the public interest are seen as of importance in dealing with the crime of perjury. It is perceived as a crime which strikes at the very roots of the rule of law and the administration of justice.[20]

Practice.

Hagen v. H.M. Advocate
1983 S.C.C.R. 245
(Lord Justice-General Emslie, Lords Cameron and Avonside)

A 17-year-old youth pled guilty to committing perjury at a trial of a person on charges including attempted rape. Having given statements earlier to the police incriminating that person, in giving evidence he denied having made them. The person on trial had been convicted on other evidence. The appellant was sentenced to four years' detention.

Sentence: the crime of perjury struck at the very roots of the rule of law and the administration of justice; however, it had since come to light that at the time the appellant had been subjected to intimidation and violence and in view of this and of his age, the sentence was quashed and three years' detention substituted.

Gordon v. Hamilton
1987 S.C.C.R. 146
(Lord Justice-General Emslie, Lords Grieve and Kincraig)

A 17-year-old first offender pled guilty to committing perjury when he had denied in an assault trial making a statement to police officers inculpating the accused. He was sentenced to three months' detention.

Sentence: since his conviction the appellant had obtained employment and would have been able to pay a fine; the sentence was quashed and a fine of £500 substituted.

9.24   Perverting the course of justice
9.24.1   Attempt to pervert the course of justice.

MacLean v. Mackenzie
1986 S.C.C.R. 482
(Lord Justice-Clerk Ross, Lords Robertson and Dunpark)

A 39-year-old first offender was convicted of attempting to

pervert the course of justice by making telephone calls threatening witnesses in a forthcoming trial. She was sentenced to 60 days' imprisonment.

Sentence: it was significant that all four witnesses telephoned were very worried at what had happened and the sentence was upheld.

Davidson v. *H.M. Advocate*
1990 S.C.C.R. 699
(Lord Justice-Clerk Ross, Lords Murray and Weir)

The appellant was convicted of attempting to pervert the course of justice by making false statements to police officers, providing a false alibi. He was sentenced to 12 months' imprisonment.

Sentence: the appellant had only maintained his false alibi for one day and so there was no serious waste of police time; the sentence was quashed and six months' imprisonment imposed.

9.25 Prison breaking

Salmon v. *H.M. Advocate*
1991 S.C.C.R. 628
(Lords Allanbridge, Morison and McDonald)

The appellant pled guilty to escaping from prison while serving a five-year sentence. The sheriff based his sentence on the amount of remission which the appellant would have received, modified that to take account of mitigating factors and arrived at a sentence of 20 months' imprisonment, consecutive to the original sentence.

Sentence: the sheriff's approach was wrong; the court should consider all the circumstances of the offence and not carry out calculations based on possible periods of remission; the sentence was quashed and one of 12 months' imprisonment imposed, consecutive to the original sentence.

9.26 Rape

9.26.1 Rape.

Conlon v. *H.M. Advocate*
1981 S.C.C.R. 141
(Lord Justice-General Emslie, Lords Cameron and Stott)

After the victim, a 21-year-old girl, had given her evidence and been cross-examined, the appellant pled guilty to jumping out on her while she had been walking along a lane shortly after 10 pm. He had seized her by the throat, threatened to kill her and raped her twice. The appellant, aged 27, had not previously been in prison but had nine previous convictions for violence and possession of offensive weapons. He was sentenced to eight years' imprisonment.

Sentence: upheld, falling within the upper range of sentences appropriate for bad crimes of rape but being fully merited, the trial judge describing this as one of the worst crimes of rape with which he had had to deal.

Townsley v. *H.M. Advocate*
1986 S.C.C.R. 248
(Lord Justice-General Emslie, Lords Grieve and Avonside)

An offender with previous convictions for abduction, rape and other offences involving sexual violence pled guilty to a charge of rape. He expressed the earnest wish to undergo treatment to bring his sexual urges under control. He was sentenced to life imprisonment.

Sentence: the psychiatric assessment of his condition would be an important factor in determining his release date and the sentence was upheld; the sentence was not only the correct one but the best one in the public interest and in the interest of the appellant himself.

9.26.2   Attempted rape.
Allan v. *H.M. Advocate*
1983 S.C.C.R. 183
(Lord Justice-General Emslie, Lords Cameron and Avonside)

The appellant pled guilty to assault with intent to rape and attempted rape of a 27-year-old nursing sister. Four psychiatrists gave conflicting evidence as to the appropriateness of a hospital order. As the offender had not been shown to be suffering from mental disorder and as no bed was available for him at the state hospital, taking account of the circumstances of the offence and his record the trial judge considered a life sentence to be appropriate.

Sentence: upheld, life imprisonment being the most humane disposal available to the court and not being inimical to the best interests of the appellant; the sentence was subject to review from time to time and could be terminated by the grant of licence should psychiatric treatment and examination permit.

9.27 Reset

9.27.1 Reset of a shotgun.

Bennett v. *Tudhope*
1987 S.C.C.R. 203
(Lord Justice-Clerk Ross, Lords Robertson and Dunpark)

A first offender was convicted of resetting a shotgun and was sentenced to three months' imprisonment.

Sentence: it was very important that a stolen shotgun should not be capable of falling into the wrong hands and the sentence was upheld.

9.27.2 Reset of wheels and tyres.

Bowman v. *MacDougall*
1987 S.C.C.R. 14
(Lord Justice-Clerk Ross, Lords Robertson and Dunpark)

A haulage contractor reset four wheels and tyres with a second-hand value of £980. He had paid £240 for them. He was fined £1,500.

Sentence: the offence was a serious one and any penalty must be sufficient to deter the appellant and others from engaging in similar activities but must also bear some relation to the nature of the particular offence; the fine was quashed and a fine of £750 imposed.

9.28 Road Traffic

9.28.1 Causing death by reckless/dangerous driving.

Maximum sentence. The maximum sentence which may be imposed should normally be confined to cases which might be regarded as the worst possible cases of this kind.[21]

Causing death by reckless driving and driving with an excess of alcohol. Where a person was convicted of causing death by reckless driving and driving with an excess of alcohol and the reckless driving charge made no reference to drink, the judge should not take account of the excess of alcohol in sentencing on the reckless driving charge. It would appear that the correct procedure would be to impose a sentence on the reckless driving charge without taking account of the drinking and a separate sentence on the drink charge without taking account of the manner of driving and, if the sentences were custodial, to make them consecutive.[22] Similar considerations would apply in respect of dangerous driving.

Practice.

Earnshaw v. H.M. Advocate
1982 J.C. 11; 1981 S.C.C.R. 279; 1982 S.L.T. 179
(Lord Justice-General Emslie, Lords Avonside and Jauncey)

The appellant was convicted of causing death by reckless driving. He had driven an articulated lorry downhill at a speed which prevented him from retaining control of it. At a bend the lorry jack-knifed and collided with a car, causing the death of the three occupants of the car. The trial judge imposed the maximum sentence of five years' imprisonment and a ten year disqualification from driving.

Sentence: the measure of recklessness was the speed at which the lorry entered the bend in damp road conditions; the speed in this instance had been just above that at which control would be lost, so that the recklessness was not of the highest degree; and prison sentence reduced to three years.

Cooper v. H.M. Advocate
1982 S.C.C.R. 87
(Lord Justice-General Emslie, Lords Cameron and Stott)

A motorcyclist was charged with causing the death of another person by driving recklessly at excessive speed and while his driving was impaired by drink. There was evidence of his blood alcohol level of 113 mg of alcohol in 100 ml of blood but no evidence as to the significance of that figure. The sheriff directed the jury to delete the reference to impairment. On conviction, in imposing sentence the sheriff took into account the "drink factor" and imposed a sentence of 12 months' imprisonment and disqualified him for six years.

Sentence: after impairment by drink had been deleted from the libel, drink ceased to be a relevant factor; and sentence of imprisonment quashed and fine of £1,000 substituted.

Salusbury-Hughes v. *H.M. Advocate*
1987 S.C.C.R. 38
(Lord Justice-Clerk Ross, Lords Robertson and Avonside)

A 25-year-old man with no significant previous convictions was convicted of causing death by reckless driving. He had approached a dangerous bend at a speed between 60 and 80 mph, crossed to the wrong side of the road and collided with another car, killing one of his own passengers and injuring everyone else. He was sentenced to four months' imprisonment.

Sentence: upheld, having regard to the gravity of the offence.

Anderson v. *H.M. Advocate*
1987 S.C.C.R. 529
(Lord Justice-Clerk Ross, Lords McDonald and Wylie)

A 23-year-old was convicted of causing the death of a friend, who was a passenger in his car. He had driven at speeds in excess of 100 mph as a result of which he lost control of the car, which had travelled along the top of a dyke and overturned. He was sentenced to nine months' imprisonment.

Sentence: the only appropriate disposal was a custodial sentence but the sentence was quashed and six months' imprisonment imposed.

Shields v. *H.M. Advocate*
1987 S.C.C.R. 706
(Lord Justice-Clerk Ross, Lords Dunpark and McDonald)

A man was convicted of causing death by reckless driving. He had driven at speeds of up to 60 mph, in a built-up area, failed to take a bend, crossed to the other side of the road and struck and killed a pedestrian. He was sentenced to five years' imprisonment, the maximum sentence.

Sentence: although the driving was deplorable, the circumstances of the offence and the personal circumstances of the appellant did not warrant the maximum sentence; the sentence was quashed and three years' imprisonment imposed.[23]

Douglas v. *H.M. Advocate*
1990 S.C.C.R. 188; 1990 S.L.T. 781
(Lord Justice-General Hope, Lords Cowie and Morison)

The appellant was convicted of causing death by reckless driving. He had overtaken a lorry in bad weather and collided with an oncoming car when on the wrong side of the road. He was sentenced to 12 months' imprisonment.

Sentence: the sheriff had proceeded upon the basis that this was an example of recklessness at the upper end of the scale of such conduct but was not justified in so doing, the recklessness not being deliberate; the sentence was quashed and six months' imprisonment substituted.

Ross v. *H.M. Advocate*
1991 S.C.C.R. 781
(Lord Justice-General Hope, Lords Allanbridge and Cowie)

The appellant was convicted of two incidents of reckless driving. The first involved an attempt to overtake in the face of an oncoming vehicle; the second involved negotiating a bend at excessive speed and colliding with an oncoming car, resulting in the death of two of the passengers. He was sentenced to one year's imprisonment.

Sentence: upheld; the sheriff, who had heard all the evidence and was in the best position to assess the gravity of the offence, was acting well within the limits of his discretion in deciding that a substantial custodial sentence was necessary.

Russell v. *H.M. Advocate*
1991 S.C.C.R. 790
(Lord Justice-General Hope, Lords Allanbridge and Grieve)

A 19-year-old first offender was convicted of causing the death of a 12-year-old girl in a built-up area. A car driven by him at a speed in excess of 58 mph struck her as she was crossing the road. He was sentenced to one year's detention and disqualified from driving for five years and until he passed a driving test.

Sentence: sentence of detention upheld; this was not only a serious case of reckless driving but the appellant's gross recklessness caused the death of a young child; but no good purpose would be served by such a long period of disqualification, which was quashed along with the order to resit the test and a disqualification of two years was substituted.

Causing death by dangerous driving. On the implementation of s. 1 of the Road Traffic Act 1991 on 1 July 1992, the offence of causing death by reckless driving was replaced by that of causing death by dangerous driving.

9.28.2   Reckless/dangerous driving.

Practice.

Campbell v. *Johnston*
1981 S.C.C.R. 179
(Lord Justice-General Emslie, Lords Stott and Dunpark)

The appellant pled guilty to two charges of reckless driving and one of driving with excess alcohol in his body. The second incident of reckless driving was committed in an endeavour to avoid a pursuing police car. He earned £100 per week. He was fined £75 and £500 on the reckless driving charges and £80 on the drink driving charge and disqualified for two years and until he passed a driving test.

Sentence: upheld, and sheriff congratulated on his selection of penalties.[24]

Connorton v. *Annan*
1981 S.C.C.R. 307
(Lord Justice-General Emslie, Lords Cameron and Stott)

The appellant was convicted of reckless driving. After an altercation, he was set upon by a group and he attempted to drive off in his car but was impeded from doing so by two youths, one of whom kicked his car. He drove along the pavement towards eight other associated youths who leapt out of the way and he collided with a motorcycle which fell over onto one of them. The sheriff treated the offence as a serious one and imposed a fine of £200 and a disqualification for one year, although this would have entailed the appellant losing his job as a television mechanic. No appeal against conviction was taken.

Sentence: the reason for the commission of the offence was the need to escape from a dangerous situation; as the appellant would lose his employment and as this was not a serious case of reckless driving, the fine and disqualification were quashed and an admonition was substituted.

Morrison v. *Valentine*
1990 S.C.C.R. 692
(Lord Justice-Clerk Ross, Lords Murray and McDonald)

The appellant drove off after a man had punched the door of his locked car, trying to enter it. The man mounted the bonnet of the car in an attempt to stop him. The appellant drove on for 30 yards when, at a sharp bend, the man slid off. He was convicted of reckless driving and disqualified for six months.

Sentence: this was a highly unusual case where it was neither necessary nor appropriate to impose disqualification; the disqualification was quashed and ten penalty points imposed.

Ross v. *H.M. Advocate*
1991 S.C.C.R. 105
(Lords Allanbridge, Weir and Wylie)

The appellant pled guilty to reckless driving. He tried to escape in a stolen car from a pursuing police car, which involved a high speed chase through a residential area. He was sentenced to six months' detention, consecutive to two years' detention on theft charges.

Sentence: upheld; this was a very serious offence which might well have merited a much longer sentence and the appellant was extremely fortunate not to have the sentence increased.

Dangerous driving. On the implementation of s. 1 of the Road Traffic Act 1991 on 1 July 1992, the offence of reckless driving was replaced by that of dangerous driving.

9.28.3 Careless driving.

General. The consequences of an incident of careless driving are not necessarily irrelevant, since they may indicate that a person's driving fell below the standard to be expected of a careful and competent driver. They may illustrate the gravity and degree of the breach of the statutory provision. However, in a charge restricted solely to careless driving, the fact that a person was killed as a result of the careless driving is not relevant so far as sentence is concerned. The unforeseen and unexpected results of the carelessness are not in themselves relevant to penalty.[25]

It is therefore not the case that the consequences of a course of driving are irrelevant considerations in determining whether or not someone has in fact been guilty of careless or reckless driving. If it is relevant to guilt that careless driving was bad enough to result in personal injury, it is presumably also relevant to sentence.[26]

The fact that a person is a professional driver or is the driver of a large vehicle makes no difference to the standard of driving required. There is no double standard requiring, for example, a professional lorry driver to demonstrate an above-average standard of driving.[27]

Practice.

King v. Cardle
1981 S.C.C.R. 22
(Lord Justice-General Emslie, Lords Cameron and Stott)

A bus driver was convicted of careless driving after his vehicle overtook and then collided with another bus. The sheriff viewed this as a very bad case of careless driving, which could well be described as dangerous driving, and fined him £60 and disqualified him for three months.

Sentence: this was not a very serious collision; the sheriff was wrong to treat it as being on the borderline between careless and reckless driving; and disqualification quashed.

Tariq v. Carmichael
1982 S.C.C.R. 488
(Lord Justice-General Emslie, Lords Cameron and Wylie)

Due to a lapse of attention a driver allowed his car to cross onto the wrong side of the road where it collided with an oncoming vehicle. The sheriff fined him £75, disqualified him for six months and ordered him to resit a driving test.

Sentence: the appeal against disqualification was dismissed; but a single instance of a lapse of attention, even to a gross degree, did not necessarily bring into question the driver's competence to drive and call for the imposition of an order to resit the test; and the order to resit the test was recalled.

Dunlop v. Allan
1984 S.C.C.R. 329
(Lord Justice-General Emslie, Lord Justice-Clerk Wheatley and Lord Ross)

A bus driver with a clean record was convicted of careless driving. He failed to see a motor cyclist and collided with him as a result of which he was killed. In addition to being fined he was disqualified for six months.

Sentence: when the circumstances of the offence and of the offender were properly weighed in the balance, disqualification was an excessive penalty and it was quashed.

Melville v. Lockhart
1985 S.C.C.R. 242
(Lord Justice-General Emslie, Lords Cameron and Brand)

A 23-year-old first offender drove carelessly at up to 80 mph in a 40 mph limit, failed to stop when directed to do so by a police officer and drove on the wrong side of the road. He was fined £250 and disqualified for three years.

Sentence: upheld; an act of such total irresponsibility justified giving to the public some protection against the possibility of a recurrence.

Malpas v. Hamilton
1988 S.C.C.R. 546
(Lords Brand, Morison and Weir)

A first offender was convicted of careless driving after she had struck and killed a pedestrian with her car. She was fined £200 and disqualified for six months.

Sentence: it is only in a more than usually serious case of careless driving that disqualification should be imposed; the disqualification was quashed and five penalty points imposed.

McCrone v. *Normand*
1988 S.C.C.R. 551; 1989 S.L.T. 332
(Lord Justice-Clerk Ross, Lords Dunpark and McDonald)

A man was convicted of careless driving after reversing a mobile shop in an area used as a children's playground, striking and killing a child who had been playing behind his vehicle. He was fined £400 and had his licence endorsed.

Sentence: the fine was quashed and a £100 fine imposed.

Owens v. *McNaughtan*
1990 S.C.C.R. 355
(Lords Cowie, Sutherland and McDonald)

An appellant with a free income of £100 per week and a clean driving licence pled guilty to careless driving. He had lost control of the car on a left-hand bend in bad weather and collided with two cars on the opposite side of the road. He was fined £500 and had nine penalty points endorsed on his licence, the maximum number.

Sentence: the fine was upheld but the penalty points were quashed and seven substituted.

9.28.4 Alcohol.

Nature of the driving. If an offender is charged solely with driving with an excess of alcohol, the Crown should not elaborate on the manner of the driving or the judge may have difficulty in putting this information out of his mind altogether. The nature of the driving would not be a relevant consideration in sentencing an offender for driving with an excess of alcohol.[28]

Special campaign. The existence of a government-sponsored publicity campaign over the Christmas and New Year period warning the public of the dangers of drinking and driving does not justify the imposition of severe penalties in order to support and strengthen it. The courts have a duty to impose an appropriate penalty at whatever time of year an offence may be committed.[29]

Driving with an excess of alcohol.

Whyte v. Hogg
(1975) S.C.C.R. Supp. 100
(Lord Justice-Clerk Wheatley, Lords Kissen and Thomson)

The appellant pled guilty to driving with a level of 314 mg of alcohol per 100 ml of blood, nearly four times the permitted limit. One week earlier he had been disqualified for two years and ordered to resit a driving test for a similar offence and he was an unreformed alcoholic. The sheriff disqualified him for life.

Sentence: upheld.

Beattie v. Ingram
1986 S.C.C.R. 38
(Lord Justice-General Emslie, Lords Grieve and Kincraig)

A person with no previous road traffic convictions but with a serious drink problem pled guilty to driving with 90 mg of alcohol in 100 ml of blood. He was disqualified for life.

Sentence: it was not necessary in the public interest to disqualify the appellant for life, although a fairly long period of disqualification was called for to enable him to cure himself; the disqualification was quashed and a six years' disqualification imposed.

Donnelly v. Hamilton
1987 S.C.C.R. 313
(Lord Justice-Clerk Ross, Lords McDonald and Kincraig)

A 53-year-old first offender pled guilty to driving with 158 mg of alcohol per 100 ml of blood and was convicted of careless driving. He was sentenced to three months' imprisonment on the drink charge on the basis that he had consciously driven after consuming a considerable quantity of alcohol, leading him to lose control of his car with foreseeable consequences.

Sentence: upheld.

Shirlaw v. Wilson
1988 S.C.C.R. 225
(Lords Grieve, Wylie and Sutherland)

A man pled guilty to driving with a level of 120 mg of alcohol per 100 ml of breath. He had an analogous 13-year-old previous conviction. He was sentenced to three months' imprisonment and disqualified for four years.

Sentence: quashed and a £750 fine and three years' disqualification imposed.

Lockerby v. *MacDougall*
1988 S.C.C.R. 471
(Lord Justice-Clerk Ross, Lords Wylie and Kincraig)

A man pled guilty to driving with 54 mg of alcohol per 100 ml of breath. He had a previous analogous conviction just over 10 years earlier. He was unemployed with a family of five. He was fined £300 and disqualified for two years.

Sentence: the fine was quashed and a £200 fine imposed; the level of alcohol was not so high as to justify two years' disqualification, which was quashed, and one year substituted.[30]

Third conviction.

Marshall v. *Carmichael*
1990 S.C.C.R. 58
(Lords Brand, Murray and McDonald)

The appellant pled guilty to driving a van with a proportion of 109 mg of alcohol per 100 ml of breath. He had analogous previous convictions in 1973 and 1976. He had only driven the van a short distance because the window was broken and he was afraid that it might be stolen. He was sentenced to six months' imprisonment.

Sentence: the appellant had avoided road traffic offences for an appreciable period; the sentence was quashed and 150 hours' community service imposed.

Giordano v. *Carmichael*
1990 S.C.C.R. 61
(Lord Justice-Clerk Ross, Lords Dunpark and Wylie)

The appellant pled guilty to driving with a level of 220 mg of alcohol per 100 ml of blood. She had analogous previous convictions in 1981 and 1983. She was sentenced to 60 days' imprisonment.

Sentence: since this was the third conviction within ten years and the appellant was almost three times over the prescribed limit, the sheriff was fully entitled to conclude that a custodial sentence was required and the sentence was upheld.

Cairns v. McLeod
1992 S.C.C.R. 787
(Lords Allanbridge, Cullen and Wylie)

A man pled guilty to driving with a level of 103 mg of alcohol per 100 ml of breath. He had two analogous previous convictions. He was sentenced to two months' imprisonment, disqualified for five years and ordered to resit a driving test.

Sentence: while making no criticism of the sheriff, there was an appropriate alternative sentence in the special circumstances of this case; sentence quashed and 200 hours' community service imposed.

In charge of motor vehicle.

Harper v. Lees
1992 S.C.C.R. 7
(Lords Cowie, Grieve and Brand)

The appellant was found asleep, with an excess of alcohol, slumped over the wheel of his car which was parked half-a-mile from his home. He was fined £150 and disqualified for a year.

Sentence: the disqualification was quashed and 10 penalty points imposed.

9.28.5 Failure to provide specimen.

General. The Court of Criminal Appeal has stated that it has become apparent that the courts must take a strong and firm view about people who drive, either under the influence of drink or in a situation where they refuse to give specimens.[31]

Practice.

McParland v. Wilson
1988 S.C.C.R. 158
(Lords Brand, Prosser and Kincraig)

A first offender pled guilty to failing to provide specimens of breath for analysis and was sentenced to three months' imprisonment.

Sentence: a sentence of imprisonment for a first offender in respect of this charge was inappropriate; the sentence was quashed and a fine of £100 imposed.

Note: Dicta in this case was subsequently disapproved in *Hawthorn* v. *Jessop* 1991 S.C.C.R. 674.

Weddle v. *Carmichael*
1991 S.C.C.R. 64
(Lords Allanbridge, Kincraig and Brand)

The appellant pled guilty to failing to provide specimens for analysis and admitted two analogous previous convictions. He was married with three children, earning £23,000 per year. He was sentenced to three months' imprisonment.

Sentence: upheld.

Hawthorn v. *Jessop*
1991 S.C.C.R. 674
(Lord Justice-General Hope, Lords Allanbridge, Murray, Morison and Brand)

The appellant was convicted of failing to provide specimens of breath for analysis. Evidence of the manner of driving and degree of intoxication was led at the trial. As the appellant was manifestly drunk he was fined £150 and disqualified for three years.

Sentence: upheld; an offender should not be able to escape the consequences of providing a specimen by refusing to provide one and there was no good reason why the court should not take account of evidence about the degree of impairment where a specimen was refused.

9.28.6 Failure to provide roadside breath test.

MacMillan v. *Scott*
1988 S.C.C.R. 219
(Lords Grieve, Wylie and Sutherland)

A driver pled guilty to failing to provide a specimen of breath for a roadside test. He was fined £100 and disqualified for six months.

Sentence: the disqualification was quashed and four penalty points imposed.

9.28.7   Failure to stop.

General. In sentencing a driver for failing to stop and give his particulars after an accident, a sheriff is not entitled to draw the inference that the driver was trying to escape the consequences of some more serious traffic offence, such as driving under the influence of an excessive amount of alcohol, where there is nothing to warrant such a view and which would therefore be mere speculation.[32]

In a later decision the appeal court has gone further and has indicated that it was irrelevant to a charge of failing to stop that a driver left the scene of an accident with the sole purpose of avoiding the obvious consequences (of drink driving) should the police have become involved. The sentence should therefore not reflect this irrelevant consideration.[33]

Practice.

Lawson v. *Ingram*
1981 S.C.C.R. 240
(Lord Justice-Clerk Wheatley, Lords Stott and Dunpark)

The appellant failed to stop and give his particulars after a slight accident. He had pointed out his number-plate ("1 DAL") to the other driver and driven off, wrongly thinking that the other driver had recognised him. He was fined £30 and disqualified for six months.

Sentence: as the accident was slight and the appellant had stopped and given some information which could have led to his being identified, the disqualification was quashed.

Jackson v. *Smith*
1982 S.C.C.R. 138
(Lord Justice-Clerk Wheatley, Lords Hunter and Robertson)

After a minor accident a disabled driver with a clean record for over four years failed to stop. The sheriff disqualified him for six months.

Sentence: having regard to the minor nature of the accident, the driver's clean record for the previous four years, his medical condition which pointed to his need to be able to drive and the testimonials which were provided, the court was justified in interfering with the sentence; and disqualification quashed.

Paterson v. *MacNeill*
1982 S.C.C.R. 141
(Lord Justice-Clerk Wheatley, Lords Hunter and Robertson)

After being involved in a road accident, the appellant ran off and then drove past the scene in a friend's vehicle without stopping. He had no previous convictions. He was disqualified for six months.

Sentence: as this was an offence which had become so prevalent in the area that the public's attention had frequently been drawn to the fact that it might well result in disqualification, the sheriff was entitled to disqualify.

Croll v. *Smith*
1982 S.C.C.R. 292
(Lord Justice-General Emslie, Lords Cameron and Avonside)

The appellant failed to stop after running his car into a wall. He was disqualified for six months.

Sentence: upheld; the sheriff was entitled to treat the offence as a serious one deserving a punishment which would mark the conduct of the driver.

Livingstone v. *Smith*
1988 S.C.C.R. 468
(Lord Justice-Clerk Ross, Lords Wylie and Kincraig)

A 19-year-old employed driver failed to stop when his car collided with a stationary car, causing slight damage to both vehicles. He was fined £75 and had eight penalty points imposed, which meant that he was disqualified under the totting-up provisions.

Sentence: the appropriate number of penalty points was five, the minimum number available; since the penalty points were reduced, the fine was increased and the fine was quashed and one of £150 imposed.

9.28.8   Failure to stop and failure to report.

General. Where a person drove carelessly whereupon a man was killed, failed to stop and failed to report the accident, the appeal court has indicated that the gravest of the three offences calling for the stiffest penalty was the failure to report.[34]

Practice.

Morrison v. Haughney
1984 S.C.C.R. 315
(Lord Justice-General Emslie, Lord Justice-Clerk Wheatley and Lord Ross)

An appellant pled guilty to careless driving consequent upon which a drunk man lying on the road had been killed, failing to stop and failing to report the accident, at first denying to police officers making investigations that he had been involved. The sheriff fined him £400, £1,000 and £100 respectively and disqualified him for life for failing to stop, on the basis that someone who was so morally defective and so regardless of his fellow-beings should not be permitted to drive.

Sentence: (1) the penalty for careless driving was upheld;
(2) considerations of morality were irrelevant in fixing a penalty for contravention of a statutory provision, the object of which was the provision of information; and sentence for failing to stop quashed and fine of £100 imposed; and
(3) the failure to report was the gravest of the three charges and the sentence imposed was inadequate; and sentence quashed and £500 fine and three years disqualification substituted.

9.28.9 Driving while disqualified. The Court of Criminal Appeal has questioned whether in general the penalties for driving while disqualified are adequate.[35]

9.28.10 Driving without lights, failure to stop for police and driving with an excess of alcohol.

Gatens v. Wilson
1985 S.C.C.R. 47
(Lord Justice-General Emslie, Lords Cameron and Brand)

The appellant pled guilty to driving without lights, failing to stop when signalled to do so by police officers and driving with 112 mg of alcohol in 100 ml of breath. He was unemployed but had good prospects of employment. He was fined £100, £100 and £500 respectively and disqualified on the drink charge.

Sentence: upheld; although the fines were substantial, that was another matter from them being excessive.

9.28.11 Insurance.

General. Driving without insurance has been described as a particularly serious offence which might have very serious consequences for the public.[36] However, for the normal case penalty points should generally be applied.[37]

Practice.

Reid v. *McLeod*

1984 S.C.C.R. 333

(Lord Justice-General Emslie, Lord Justice-Clerk Wheatley and Lord Ross)

An appellant pled guilty to driving without insurance. He was fined £100 and disqualified for six months.

Sentence: upheld, offences of driving without insurance being particularly serious ones which may have very serious consequences for the public.

Gibb v. *McGlennan*

1990 S.C.C.R. 759

(Lords Wylie, McDonald and Brand)

The appellant pled guilty to driving without insurance and was disqualified for 12 months.

Sentence: the sheriff was not justified in imposing a disqualification of 12 months for a failure to have insurance, serious as such a charge was; Parliament had provided for a range of six to eight penalty points for this offence; the disqualification was quashed and six penalty points imposed.

9.28.12 Speeding.

General.

Taylor v. *Cardle*

1988 S.C.C.R. 450

(Lords Grieve, Avonside and Kincraig)

After driving at 58 mph in a 30 mph limit, the appellant failed to pay the fixed penalty offered to him. He had one previous analogous conviction in 1983. He was fined £280.

Sentence: upheld.

Longmuir v. *Carmichael*
1990 S.C.C.R. 522
(Lords Cowie, Morison and Weir)

The appellant pled guilty to driving at 47 mph in a 30 mph limit. He had two previous convictions for speeding which had resulted in six penalty points being endorsed on his licence. He was fined £50 and disqualified for six months.

Sentence: Parliament had laid down that in the normal case for a speeding offence a fine and penalty points would be appropriate unless the number of penalty points which appeared on the licence exceeded 12; the disqualification was quashed and three penalty points imposed.

Murray v. *McGlennan*
1991 S.C.C.R. 18
(Lord Justice-Clerk Ross, Lords McDonald and Brand)

A first offender earning £177 per week pled guilty to driving at 85 mph on a road with a 60 mph speed limit. The sheriff stated that speeding was rife on this stretch of the road and fined him £250.

Sentence: upheld.

Patrick v. *McGlennan*
1991 S.C.C.R. 100
(Lords Allanbridge, Sutherland and Weir)

A first offender pled guilty to driving at 73 mph on a road where the speed limit was 50 mph. The justice took into account two recent fatal accidents there and fined him £250.

Sentence: while a judge may take into account local knowledge, that must be done with discretion and moderation; the sentence was quashed and a fine of £75 was imposed.

Fifth offence.

Briggs v. *Guild*
1987 S.C.C.R. 141
(Lord Justice-General Emslie, Lords Grieve and Kincraig)

A driver was convicted of his fifth speeding offence and fined £20 with three penalty points imposed.

Sentence: an appropriate penalty would be £400; the fine was quashed and a fine of £400 imposed.

A74.

Perryman v. *MacDougall*

1988 S.C.C.R. 24

(Lord Justice-Clerk Ross, Lords McDonald and Hunter)

The appellant pled guilty to driving at 107 mph on a part of the A74 where the speed limit was 70 mph. He was fined £100 and disqualified for six months.

Sentence: the A74 was a notoriously dangerous road, the speed was grossly excessive and a period of disqualification was fully justified, but the disqualification was quashed and three months' disqualification imposed.

Clark v. *MacDougall*

1988 S.C.C.R. 53

(Lord Justice-General Emslie, Lords Brand and Allanbridge)

The appellant pled guilty to driving at 110 mph on a part of the A74 where the speed limit was 70 mph. He was a first offender employing 15 people and required his licence for his business. He was fined £100 and disqualified for three months.

Sentence: the consequences to the appellant and his dependants of a short period of disqualification would have been out of all proportion to any supposed advantage to the public interest which it may have; the disqualification was quashed and three penalty points imposed.

9.28.13 Taking and driving away.

McAngus v. *Hingston*

1990 S.C.C.R. 547

(Lords Wylie, Cowie and Brand)

A first offender pled guilty to attempting to take and drive away a van. He was fined £150 and disqualified for a year.

Sentence: the circumstances of this particular offence were deplorable and were appropriately visited by a monetary penalty; there was no reason to impose a disqualification, which was quashed, and the mandatory eight penalty points were imposed.

9.28.14 Construction and use.

Overweight lorries.

Patterson v. *Walkingshaw*
1989 S.C.C.R. 283
(Lords Brand, Coulsfield and Milligan)

The owner of a lorry driven from Northern Ireland to Scotland pled guilty to four offences of using the lorry while it was overweight. He was fined a total of £1,450.

Sentence: upheld.

Montgomery Transport Ltd. v. *Walkingshaw*
1992 S.C.C.R. 17
(Lord Justice-Clerk Ross, Lords Murray and Morison)

A company was fined £1,000 for each of two offences and the drivers were fined £200 and £250 in respect of lorries which were 3.6 per cent and 4.9 per cent overweight.

Sentences: upheld.

9.29 Robbery

9.29.1 Medical profession. The Court of Criminal Appeal has indicated that it should be clearly understood that anyone who resorts to assault and robbery against members of the medical profession cannot expect to be treated with any leniency by the courts.[38]

9.29.2 Armed robbery.

Davidson and Anr. v. *H.M. Advocate*
1981 S.C.C.R. 371
(Lord Justice-General Emslie, Lords Avonside and Jauncey)

The appellant Davidson was convicted of armed robbery committed with sawn-off shotguns, one of which was loaded, and a bayonet, in which over £4,500 was stolen. He had a long criminal record. The trial judge imposed a sentence of 14 years' imprisonment.

Sentence: the trial judge had adopted the correct approach in imposing a very substantial sentence which was merited in the public interest but the sentence imposed was excessive; and sentence reduced to 11 years' imprisonment.

9.29.3 Assault and robbery.

Reilly v. *H.M. Advocate*
1983 S.C.C.R. 311
(Lord Justice-General Emslie, Lords Cameron and Avonside)

A 55-year-old man carried out two hold-ups in building society offices within two weeks of each other. He pretended to have a bomb which he threatened to explode. On the second occasion he obtained £100. He was virtually a first offender and his personality had disintegrated following the loss of a job through drink and following an addiction to drink and gambling. He was sentenced to 30 months' imprisonment.

Sentence: crimes of this kind will almost in every case result in a custodial sentence; in the light of the mitigating circumstances and upon the view that the crimes were pathetically approached and pathetically executed and that the appellant was a man who perhaps deserved sympathy, the sentence was quashed and a sentence of 18 months' imprisonment substituted.

McIntyre v. *H.M. Advocate*
1989 S.C.C.R. 34
(Lords Brand, Sutherland and Coulsfield)

Along with a co-accused, an appellant pled guilty to assault and robbery by luring a doctor to a common close by making a false telephone call saying that a patient needed his attendance in the tenement. Masked, they threatened him with sticks and demanded his medical bags, which he handed over. He was sentenced to seven years' imprisonment.

Sentence: upheld, and with some reluctance and hesitation it was not increased.

Curran v. *Jessop*
1991 S.C.C.R. 150
(Lord Justice-Clerk Ross, Lords Cameron of Lochbroom and Grieve)

A 16-year-old who was a first offender before the courts pled guilty to assaulting and robbing three younger boys who were pulled by the hair and ear, threatened with a bottle and robbed of two watches. The social enquiry report revealed a long history of bad behaviour and offending. He was sentenced to three months' detention.

Sentence: upheld.

Lannan v. *H.M. Advocate*
1991 S.C.C.R. 969
(Lords Allanbridge, Brand and Wylie)

A first offender pled guilty to assault and robbery in a corner shop. Masked, he and his co-accused threatened employees with a knife and obtained £230. As such shops appeared to be soft targets for robberies, a deterrent exemplary sentence of three years' imprisonment was imposed.

Sentence: upheld.

Willets v. *H.M. Advocate*
1991 S.C.C.R. 976
(Lords Allanbridge, Brand and Wylie)

Two first offenders aged 15 and 16 at the time of the offence pled guilty to threatening a shopkeeper with a replica handgun and a hammer and robbing her of £20. They were sentenced to 18 months' detention and to an additional six months' detention on a firearms charge.

Sentence: upheld; these types of crime were terrifying for the victim and must attract severe punishment.

9.29.4   Attempted robbery by threats.

Moore v. *H.M. Advocate*
1984 S.C.C.R. 25
(Lord Justice-General Emslie, Lords Cameron and Avonside)

After pleading guilty to attempting to rob a post office by presenting at employees there a piece of pipe which resembled a firearm, handing them a note demanding money and adopting a menacing attitude towards them, the offender was sentenced to four years' imprisonment.

Sentence: it was irrelevant for the purpose of sentence whether the offender was in possession of an actual firearm or a piece of pipe resembling a firearm; the sentence was amply justified "and indeed one could hardly have quarrelled with a longer sentence".

9.29.5 Mock robbery.

McKenzie v. *H.M. Advocate*
1983 S.C.C.R. 106
(Lord Justice-General Emslie, Lords Cameron and Stott)

A jury convicted a person of an assault at a post office by pretending that he had a firearm in his pocket and demanding money from the assistants there under threat of shooting them, but deleted from the charge that he attempted to rob them. The defence was that what had taken place was a joke. The sheriff imposed a sentence of 12 months' imprisonment.

Sentence: the jury must have accepted that there was no intention to steal behind the man's actions; his intention must have been to frighten the assistants, but only for fun; and the sentence of imprisonment which was excessive was quashed and a fine of £500 imposed.

9.30 Tax evasion

Industrial Distributions (Central Scotland) Ltd. v. *Quinn*
1984 S.C.C.R. 5; 1984 S.L.T. 240
(Lord Justice-Clerk Wheatley, Lords Hunter and Robertson)

A company failed to register for VAT. They were liable to a maximum penalty of £1,000 or three times the amount of the tax evaded, namely £21,514.44. Taking into account that they had paid £12,000 in tax after more than a year's delay, the sheriff imposed a fine of £3,000.

Sentence: in the absence of any explanation as to how the figure of £3,000 had been arrived at, it was regarded as excessive, and the sentence was quashed and a fine of £1,000 imposed.

9.31 Theft

9.31.1 Multiple shoplifting.

Selfridge v. *H.M. Advocate*
1981 S.C.C.R. 223
(Lord Justice-General Emslie, Lords Grieve and Brand)

A 43-year-old woman who was a first offender pled guilty to 16 charges of shoplifting and was sentenced to six months' imprisonment.

Sentence: such a sentence was not excessive, but in the light of further information including a medical report, sentence was deferred for six months for psychiatric treatment; and sentence of imprisonment quashed although that did not mean that a custodial sentence would not be imposed at the end of the six-month period.

9.31.2   Opening lockfast car with intent to steal.

Ketchen v. Smith
1982 S.C.C.R. 492
(Lord Justice-General Emslie, Lords Cameron and Wylie)

A 27-year-old man with nine previous convictions pled guilty to opening a lockfast car with intent to steal. He was in receipt of benefits of £21 a week. The sheriff imposed a fine of £250 and made a compensation order for £50, the cost of repairing the car, allowing three months for payment.

Sentence: the appellant's weekly benefit, even if it were all used, would be inadequate to permit him to pay £300 within three months – a contribution of £25 a week would be required and his total income was £21 a week; and fine of £50 substituted for the fine of £250.[39]

9.31.3   Theft and fraud.

White v. H.M. Advocate
1987 S.C.C.R. 73
(Lord Justice-General Emslie, Lords Robertson and Avonside)
See para. 9.18.2 *Fraud and theft*.

9.31.4   Articles recovered.

Donnelly v. Wilson
1991 S.C.C.R. 545
(Lord Justice-Clerk Ross, Lords Murray and Morison)

Two accused who were in receipt of social security benefit pled guilty to the theft of furniture valued at £1,600 which was recovered. They were fined £800 on the basis that crime should not pay and each very nearly made a profit of this amount.

Sentence: the reasoning of the sheriff did not commend itself to the appeal court; having regard to the means of the offenders the fines were excessive; the fines were quashed and fines of £150 imposed.

9.31.5 Post office theft.

Fleming-Scott v. *H.M. Advocate*
1991 S.C.C.R. 748
(Lord Justice-General Hope, Lords Allanbridge and Grieve)

A mail delivery driver pled guilty to stealing postal packets with a value of £1,500. He claimed that he had not taken the parcels for personal gain but due to pressure of work, most of them being dumped. He was the father of five children, one of whom was hydrocephalic. He was sentenced to three months' imprisonment.

Sentence: this was an offence which would normally attract a custodial sentence but in the particular circumstances of this case the sentence was quashed and one of 200 hours' community service imposed.

9.32 Tree-felling

White v. *Hamilton*
1987 S.C.C.R. 12
(Lord Justice-Clerk Ross, Lords Robertson and Dunpark)

The appellant was convicted of cutting down in breach of a tree preservation order 18 trees adjacent to his house which were blocking his view. He was aware of the order and had been warned not to cut them down. The cost of replacement had been estimated at £108,000. He was fined £1,000.

Sentence: the sheriff was clearly justified in imposing a substantial fine, which was upheld; if he had not imposed such a substantial fine others might well feel that they could contravene the provisions of tree preservation orders with impunity.

Campbell v. *Webster*
1992 S.C.C.R. 167
(Lord Justice-General Hope, Lords Allanbridge and Cowie)

The appellant was convicted of felling 550 m^3 of trees. The value of the trees was £10 per cubic metre. A fine of £5,500 was imposed.

Sentence: upheld.

9.33 Uttering

MacDonald v. *Tudhope*
1983 S.C.C.R. 341; 1984 S.L.T. 23
(Lords Cameron, Dunpark and Mayfield)

The treasurer of a police social club uttered certificates to the general secretary of the association as genuine certificates. The certificates bore to show the sums withdrawn from and the balances remaining in the club's gaming machine. He made no personal gain and the club suffered no loss, money from the machine being used for the club's trading. He was fined £500.

Sentence: as the appellant's career in the police force was in grave jeopardy, he had not misappropriated the funds and the club had suffered no loss, the sentence was quashed and an admonition was substituted.

9.34 Vandalism

Templeton v. *McLeod*
1985 J.C. 112; 1985 S.C.C.R. 357; 1986 S.L.T. 149
(Lord Justice-General Emslie, Lord Justice-Clerk Wheatley,
Lords Cameron, Robertson and Dunpark)

A single, unemployed 20-year-old with one previous conviction was convicted of damaging a pane of glass in a school window by throwing stones at it. The sheriff viewed breaking school windows as a local pastime and imposed a fine of £500.

Sentence: when there was no background of similar conduct by the offender the fine was excessive; the sentence was quashed and a £100 fine imposed.

9.35 Video cassettes

The classification system in the Video Recordings Act 1984 is designed to protect children and young persons who may otherwise be able to view work which is regarded as unsuitable for persons of their age. Accordingly, in sentencing an offender for breach of its provisions, a judge should not take into account the threat of pirate copy recordings to the legitimate video industry.[40]

9.36   Wasting police time

General. The Court of Criminal Appeal has indicated that it regards cases of wasting police time as serious ones.[41]

Practice.

Rodger v. *Wilson*

1986 S.C.C.R. 260

(Lord Justice-Clerk Ross, Lords Robertson and Dunpark)

A driver gave police officers a false story after a road accident. The sheriff took the view that this amounted to an attempt to pervert the course of justice and sentenced him to 60 days' imprisonment.

Sentence: the sheriff was not justified in treating the offence as an attempt to pervert the course of justice when it was libelled as wasting police time; the offence was a serious one and one which could not be tolerated; the sentence was quashed and a sentence of 10 days' imprisonment, backdated, imposed.

Notes

1. See para. 9.20.1.
2. *Walker* v. *H.M. Advocate* 1987 S.C.C.R. 345.
3. *Cluness* v. *Allan* 1984 S.C.C.R. 205.
4. On child kidnapping generally, see D. Kelly "Child Abduction", 1991 S.L.T. 53.
5. Contempt of Court Act 1981, s. 15(2), as amended by the Criminal Justice Act 1982, Sch. 7.
6. *Dawes* v. *Cardle* 1987 S.C.C.R. 135.
7. Parole is now competent during a period of imprisonment for contempt of court by virtue of s. 15(6) of the Contempt of Court Act 1981, as inserted by para. 19 of Sched. 1 to the Criminal Justice (Scotland) Act 1987.
8. *McLeod* v. *Allan* 1986 S.C.C.R. 666.
9. *Donnelly* v. *H.M. Advocate* 1984 S.C.C.R. 93.
10. *Mullady* v. *H.M. Advocate* 1988 S.C.C.R. 113.
11. *MacNeil* v. *H.M. Advocate* 1986 J.C. 146; 1986 S.C.C.R. 288; 1987 S.L.T. 244 (*sub nom. Socratous* v. *H.M. Advocate*).
12. *Wright* v. *Houston* 1987 S.C.C.R. 674.
13. See "Sentencing the Drug Addict", 1987 S.L.T. 340.
14. *MacNeil* v. *H.M. Advocate* 1986 J.C. 146; 1986 S.C.C.R. 288; 1987 S.L.T. 244 (*sub nom. Socratous* v. *H.M. Advocate*).
15. *Sub nom. Socratous* v. *H.M. Advocate*.
16. *Khaliq* v. *H.M. Advocate* 1984 S.C.C.R. 212.
17. 1975 Act, s. 205, as substituted by the 1980 Act, s. 43.
18. 1975 Act, s. 205A, as added by the 1980 Act, s. 43.
19. *Campbell* v. *H.M. Advocate* 1986 S.C.C.R. 516.

20. *Hagen* v. *H.M. Advocate* 1983 S.C.C.R. 245.
21. *Shields* v. *H.M. Advocate* 1987 S.C.C.R. 706.
22. *Anderson* v. *H.M. Advocate* 1987 S.C.C.R. 529.
23. It has been suggested that this case comes close to setting a tariff of three years' imprisonment for the average s. 1 case dealt with in the High Court of Justiciary: see the Commentary to the case.
24. See also *Lukey* v. *Allan* 1987 S.C.C.R. 715.
25. *McCallum* v. *Hamilton* 1986 J.C. 1; 1985 S.C.C.R. 368; 1986 S.L.T. 156; *Sharp* v. *H.M. Advocate* 1987 S.C.C.R. 179.
26. *Mundie* v. *Cardle* 1991 S.C.C.R. 118 and the Commentary thereon.
27. *Ross* v. *Houston* 1991 S.C.C.R. 102.
28. *Lindsay* v. *Jessop* 1987 S.C.C.R. 512.
29. *Liddel* v. *McNaughton* 1987 S.C.C.R. 437.
30. See also *MacPherson* v. *Ingram* 1990 S.C.C.R. 452.
31. *Weddle* v. *Carmichael* 1991 S.C.C.R. 64.
32. *Brown* v. *McLeod* 1981 S.C.C.R. 254.
33. *McNamee* v. *Carmichael* 1985 S.C.C.R. 289.
34. *Morrison* v. *Haughney* 1984 S.C.C.R. 315.
35. *Cherry* v. *Walkingshaw* 1989 S.C.C.R. 256.
36. *Reid* v. *McLeod* 1984 S.C.C.R. 333.
37. *Gibb* v. *McGlennan* 1990 S.C.C.R. 759.
38. *McIntyre* v. *H.M. Advocate* 1989 S.C.C.R. 34.
39. In ensuring that the fine imposed related to the means of the offender, the appeal court did not extend the time allowed for payment but reduced the fine.
40. *Higgins* v. *Carmichael* 1988 S.C.C.R. 17.
41. *Rodger* v. *Wilson* 1986 S.C.C.R. 260.

INDEX